THE TECHNOLOGY
ASSESSMENT
PROCESS

THE TECHNOLOGY ASSESSMENT PROCESS

A STRATEGIC FRAMEWORK FOR MANAGING TECHNICAL INNOVATION

Blake L. White

QUORUM BOOKS
NEW YORK
WESTPORT, CONNECTICUT
LONDON

Library of Congress Cataloging-in-Publication Data

White, Blake L.
    The technology assessment process : a strategic framework for
managing technical innovation / Blake L. White.
       p.   cm.
    Includes index.
    ISBN 0-89930-318-8 (lib. bdg. : alk. paper)
    1. Technology assessment.   I. Title
T174.5.W48   1988
658.5'14—dc19   88-3101

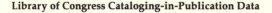

British Library Cataloguing in Publication Data is available.

Library of Congress Catalog Card Number: 88-3101
ISBN: 0-89930-318-8

First published in 1988 by Quorum Books

Greenwood Press, Inc.
88 Post Road West, Westport, Connecticut 06881

Printed in the United States of America

The paper used in this book complies with the
Permanent Paper Standard issued by the National
Information Standards Organization (Z39.48-1984).

10 9 8 7 6 5 4 3 2 1

This book is dedicated to my wife, Cheryl, for the loving support that late hours of research require; to my parents, Blake and Ruth White, for lifelong encouragement; and to my sons, Julian and Jason—may the world of the future be as unlimited as your dreams.

Contents

Figures

Preface

The Technology Assessment Process: A Strategic Framework for Managing Technical Innovation discusses key considerations and approaches to identifying opportunities for market advantage and how new technologies can be leveraged to exploit these opportunities. The benefits derived typically are reduced cost or competitive advantage or both. Though not a textbook, this volume gives valuable insight to successful rules of thumb applied by Strategic Systems, Inc. (SSI), a technology assessment consulting firm.

Admittedly, these considerations are really not rules but are examples of what works for us. No earth-shattering new buzzwords or academic concepts are revealed. However, the value of this book is its explanation of how SSI synthesized many of the popular business concepts promoted by writers and researchers, more famous than our modest staff, into a framework for decision making. We at SSI also hope to foster an understanding of the range of innovative technologies at the manager's disposal and to help the leaders of industry uncover potential applications by offering systems analysis and integration guidelines.

Most of our work has been with computer users and vendors. As such, this text is ideal for new information systems managers and internal consultants seeking to make tangible use of the myriad of computer-based products on the market today (and tomorrow). We believe it also provides value to front-line managers with profit and loss responsibility. For the reader without a technical background, we have added an appendix that gives an introduction to computers, terminology, and systems applications.

Computers will be discussed throughout this book, but no specialization in this area is required. We stress business applications, not technology for technology's sake. Therefore, the reader comfortable with publications such as *Business Week* or *The Wall Street Journal* should find *The Technology Assessment Process* just as understandable. Readers with more technical backgrounds will find this an enjoyable business applications supplement to the technologies covered by, what we in the computer industry fondly call, "trade rags."

SSI works on a confidential basis with its clients. So rather than breaking that confidence, the applications used to explain our approach are publicly discussed business cases and recent success stories. Although many computer- and communications-based applications are presented, it is our assertion that *technology assessment*, as an approach to problems, is equally valid for a wide range of technologies. Space industrialization, alternative energy sources, molecular engineering, and bioengineering are examples of multidisciplinary technologies that will influence the competitiveness of corporations in the future. Although these disciplines are not discussed here, we encourage readers to follow developments in these areas and to consider how technology assessment may be used to integrate diverse technologies into unique solutions for a broader range of business endeavors.

Fundamentally, we at SSI want you to know that technology assessment is not some new magic practiced by technical specialists. Rather, we demonstrate how success in a highly competitive world demands doing common things in an uncommon manner with the best tools and the most creative techniques available. This book provides such a management framework.

Acknowledgments

My deepest appreciation goes to Carleton Moten who provided valuable review comments and a critique of this book and for making its principles work in our practice. Special thanks to Strategic Systems' network of consultants: Kassandra Agee-Letton, Mike Brown, Brian Hurt, and Fred Toney. Margie Wells-Davis, Bob Merriweather, and Ernest Thompson of Procter & Gamble and Philip Berry at Digital Equipment—you are the best at keeping me aware of the humanistic perspective. Thanks to John Canada and Robert Llewellyn at North Carolina State, Napoleon Bryant, Dick Gruber, Stan Hedeen, Rick Bialac, and George Reynolds at Xavier University, and to Raphael Carty and Dennis King at Hewlett-Packard for guidance in the practicalities of technology.

For unselfish service, thanks to SSI's advisors: Masao Meroe, Alan Letton, Cinda Patton, Jeffrey Banks, Ron Brown, and Joe Stevenson. My gratitude also goes to Merlin and Pat Pope and the staff of Pope & Associates for introducing me to a top-notch publisher, Quorum; to Harry McKinley of Intellicom Labs and Bob Johansen of The Institute for the Future for daring to speculate; and to Dick Buten, Jim Scott, Gary Walla, Jim Reed, Jim Greensfelder, Ken Lyon, and Peter Keane at Procter & Gamble for valuable mentoring in the field of technology assessment during my career at P&G.

This work would not have been possible without the career experiences gained at Procter & Gamble and Hewlett-Packard, without the initial national exposure of our ideas by the National Technical Association (especially Janet Butler, the past president of the Cincinnati chapter of NTA), and without the guidance of Jim Dunton, Arlene Belzer, and Eric Valentine at Quorum Books.

Special acknowledgments go to those researchers, consultants, and academicians noted throughout and at the end of each chapter for the influence their works have had on the synergistic way SSI conducts business and for the impressive results of their breakthroughs, cited as examples to demonstrate our concepts. Among this group are Michael E. Porter, Richard Foster, Sherry Turkle, Alvin Toffler, John Naisbitt, Robert Fischer, Thomas Kuhn, Robert M. Bramson, Allen Harrison, Gifford Pinchot, John Rockart, Christine Bullen, Everett Rogers, Judith Larsen, Rosabeth Moss Kanter, Warren McFarlan, Robert Fano, James Botkin, Chancellor Williams, Carl Sagan, Thomas Goldstein, Michele G. Small, Joel deRosnay, Richard Telesca, William Kraus, Nicholas Weiler, Marilyn Ferguson, Fritjof Capra, James Burke, Michael Scott-Morton, Tom Allen, William Sammon, Jonathan Morell, James Leemon, Iisoo Ahn, Teresa Amabile, Bruce Berra, Bir Bhanu, Richard Snodgrass, Lauren Weinstein, Hiroyuki Watanabe, S.K.M. Wong, Wojciech Ziarko, Masaki Togai, and Nikos Troullinos.

Some of the research that has influenced SSI's approach to technology assessment comes from the following outstanding firms and institutions: McKinsey & Co., Arthur Andersen, Drexel Burnham Lambert, INQ Educational Materials Inc., Massachusetts Institute of Technology, the Center for Information Systems Research (CISR) at MIT, the Harvard Business School, Oak Ridge National Laboratory, Consultation Systems Inc., the World Future Society, Brandeis University, North Carolina A&T, Old Dominion University, Pepperdine University, the University of Minnesota, California State University, the University of Chicago, Syracuse University, Stanford University, the University of Regina, the University of North Carolina at Chapel Hill, the Institute of Electrical and Electronic Engineers (IEEE), the Institute of Industrial Engineers (IIE), the Association for Computing Machinery (ACM), and the Data Processing Management Association.

A hearty "well done" goes to those progressive companies cited for their successes and learnings. This group includes American Hospital Supply, American Airlines, Citibank, Merrill Lynch, Aetna Life & Casualty, The Clorox Company, Procter & Gamble, Johnson & Johnson, General Electric Company, MITRE, Travelers Insurance, Ford Motor Company, General Motors, Delta Airlines, Perdue Farms, McKesson, Westvaco, Schwinn Bicycle Co., Washington Mutual Savings Bank, Montgomery Ward, Rockwell International, Kidder-Peabody, General Dynamics, Pepsico, American President Lines, CBS Records, Beatrice Foods, Carnation, Motorola, Dow Jones, Wells Fargo Bank, BankAmerica Corporation, First Wachovia, Ingersoll-Rand, 3M, and the Federal Aviation Administration.

Congratulations also to the technology providers: AT&T, Advanced Micro Devices, Bell Communications Research, Bolt Beranek and Newman, Information Resources, Syntelligence, Pilot Executive Software, Alliant, Convex,

Targa Systems, Visual Communications Network, NEC, Amdahl, Hypres, Honeywell, Interleaf, Aldus, American Satellite Corporation, Houston International Teleport, SUN Microsystems, Apollo Computer, Metaphor Computer Systems, Unisys, Data General, Microsoft Corporation, Apple Computer, Xerox, Intel, INI, Ungermann-Bass, Mead Data Central, Presentation Technology, Matsushita, Nippon Telegraph and Telephone, Remote Technology, Thinking Machines Corporation, Perkin-Elmer, Siemens Information Systems, Lotus Development Corporation, Digital Equipment Corporation, Wang Laboratories, Hewlett-Packard, and IBM.

THE TECHNOLOGY
ASSESSMENT
PROCESS

1

Introduction

A NEW LOOK AT TECHNOLOGY

In today's highly competitive global economy, industry leaders are frequently looking for innovative technologies to serve as a facilitator of increased competitiveness. Strategic Systems, Inc. (SSI) proposes that, although this is certainly an appropriate path, matters be taken a step further. Regular and generous expenditures on new technologies are not enough. We believe that technology is not important for its own sake, but is important only as it affects a firm's costs, competitive advantage, industry structure, and long-term business results. Managers can no longer rest upon the luxury of a large, unfocused, and unplanned research and development budget. They can no longer merely hope that dollars devoted toward the latest technical fad will somehow benefit the organization. A *technology assessment program*, targeted at the corporate objectives and with full realization of the opportunities and constraints of the international marketplace, is a requirement.

Business executives are also finding that the relationship between technology and competitiveness is taking on a new dimension. Historically, business needs have driven technological development, but, today, the swift pace of technical change is opening up new avenues of opportunity and can be found, on occasion, driving enterprise strategies. This observation is best summarized by Harvard professor Michael E. Porter, author of *Competitive Advantage* and an acclaimed authority on competitive business strategy:

> Technological change is one of the principal drivers of competition, a great equalizer, eroding the competitive advantage of even well entrenched firms and propelling others to the forefront. Of all the things

that can change the rules of competition, technological change is among the most prominent.[1]

Why our emphasis on technology assessment as a logical, indeed a commonsense, part of doing business? Why now? Is this just another addition to the unfulfilled collection of consultants' promises such as "paperless offices" or fingertip "executive decision support"?

Definitely not! Technology assessment is a process, not a product. No one can sell it. It is a process that can be implemented by successful companies in-house. Internal assessments, however, require that firms have the good fortune and ability to spare their key technical and business managers for ongoing technology research and planning. I will outline the major considerations and approaches to technology assessment in this book, but first we must understand why such a process is needed today.

Consider that *Business Week's* 1986 forecast and Drexel Burnham Lambert's chief economist projected a long business cycle expansion with low inflation.[2] Although forecasts for 1988–1989 anticipate that growing federal deficits will put more of a strain on inflationary tendencies than expected in 1986–1987, my colleagues and I agree that lower inflation overall will force companies to accept smaller price increases. Such small increases demand strict controls on costs and productivity. SSI expects companies to look to new manufacturing, distribution, and marketing technologies coupled with advanced information systems to play crucial roles in increasing productivity and controlling costs.

According to Porter, costs, productivity, and how a company gains market share are directly related to the elements of the product's "value chain"— those activities involved in creating, producing, marketing, and delivering a product or service. Information is a permeating factor in every activity in the value chain, and technology is increasing the rate of information flow. As a result, the number of possible combinations of technologies that could be applied in the chain are increasing almost exponentially.

Information has been used to manage businesses ever since the Masai tribesman counted his herd with stick marks in the dirt. The techniques for counting have vastly improved, and the need to count has evolved to the point where businesses need not only to record transactions, but also to anticipate them. Specifically, modern computer technology was introduced to the business world in the 1950s in an effort to mirror the way accountants worked. Applications were accounting oriented and replaced highly structured paper processing tasks such as payroll, accounts payable and receivable, and general ledger. Computerization involved large corporate mainframe systems costing millions of dollars and tended by armies of computer specialists.

The next generation of systems in the 1960s was of a more operational nature. First-line managers began requesting regular structured reports on inventories, on jobs in process, and on customer credit. Later, interactive computer systems helped speed access to large databases for applications such as airline reservations and banking records.

By the 1970s, after a landmark treatise on decision support systems by Michael Scott Morton of MIT, systems consultants, designers, and managers began to see that interactive computer-based systems could be used to help solve unstructured problems and answer "what-if" questions. This opened up a new perspective on the potential of the computer, according to MIT's John Rockart and Christine Bullen, both with the university's Center for Information Systems Research (CISR).[3]

Rockart and Bullen note that in 1986 there were 15 million computer terminals and 2.1 million personal computers in use. This is up from 4.2 million terminals and 285,000 PCs just five years before. Systems now exist that allow project team members to use electronic conferencing to "meet" in computer-based interactive databases and solve problems, implement actions, and plan for the future without ever having personally met. (I know, I've done it.) Managers access external news stories and market analyses on their companies and their competitors. Private investors can look up stock prices and buy and sell securities via computers, and busy salespeople can stay in contact with the home office and other salespeople via "electronic mail." A small but growing number of senior executives are accessing corporate and external numerical data and text from PCs on their desks, at home, or via portable computers. Rockart notes that "fundamental planning and control processes of the organization are being changed as senior executives understand the computer's ability to access and assemble information concerning the ongoing operations of their firms."

All of these information technology applications, and more, have been used in many ways and by various industries to either improve the efficiency of current operations, improve the effectiveness or productivity of managers and professionals, or expand the vision of key decision makers. They have worked. We will certainly continue to invest in new technologies as a survival mechanism in a complex and competitive world. Computer and communications-related developments in areas such as artificial intelligence, expert databases, optical computers, factory automation, robotics, fiber optics, and parallel processors will continue and will be matched by unforeseen benefits of other technologies such as superconductors, molecular engineering, ceramic materials, genetic engineering, and orbital space manufacturing facilities. But, on the other hand, senior managers have heard these claims before.

Managers have been hyped on concepts such as decision support systems in the 1970s. These mainframe marvels were to give fingertip access to worldwide information banks and all of the company's records. Information was to be displayed in graphical form—no computer experience should have been needed—and the system was to have been personalized. Later versions of this same hype included such ideas as the "paperless office," the "cashless society," and a total economy based on an "Information Age." The in-house Management Information Systems (MIS) managers and the industry consultants that pushed these ideas on top management have caused a healthy skepticism to develop in these same managers. After decades of promises, top managers wonder whether the newest buzzword, "Strategic IS," is just another way for consultants to obtain contracts and MIS managers to justify higher budgets, as the editor of *Infosystems* magazine, David Freedman, explains in a recent warning to MIS managers.[4]

The sellers of these ideas prompted a backfire of expectations. Managers are asking just where these competition-killing systems are. In their zeal to promote information systems, some MIS managers and consultants forgot to explain that such efforts don't happen overnight, that strategic information systems are only as good as the level of effort put in not only by the systems staff, but also by knowledgeable line managers and end users. In an effort to position the technology in a positive light, our industry has sometimes ignored the consequences of not explaining fully that no technology is 100 percent efficient and none is likely to produce 100 percent of the desired results. There will always be shortfalls and long debugging efforts. When systems people sold the idea of a new system, sometimes the client/managers were never aware that the maintenance cost over the application system's lifetime would more than double the net present value of the development costs. Systems people know that companies never seem to have enough money for extensive designs but always come up with funds to fix a problem. As a result, they have set a bad example by just playing the numbers game and, in the process, raising false expectations.

As Freedman notes, our industry has done a super job of selling Strategic IS, but very few organizations have actually implemented it. An Arthur Andersen survey found that 97 percent of Fortune 500 IS managers believe that information systems can provide a competitive edge to their companies, but only 19 percent have implemented such systems. Only 15 percent use IS to improve customer service, and 7 percent support new product development. Echoing these findings is a similar study by Arthur Young's Glen Weekley, who says that 90 percent of his clients are interested in Strategic IS, but only 10 to 20 percent are actually pursuing it.[5]

Harvard Business Review associate editor Lynn Salerno explains some of the reasons for corporate management's hesitancy to embrace computer technology. This hesitancy caused a major slowdown in the whole computer industry in 1984–1986 that is just beginning to ease in its effects. Echoing our earlier assumptions, Salerno discusses a frustrating mismatch between expectations and performance. As a result, both users and vendors have suffered because of this gap. She notes that users couldn't get what they wanted, and computer vendors were dismayed by customers' disinterest in what the vendors had.[6]

Salerno cites problems that slowed the computer revolution. They include a rosy picture painted by over-optimistic vendors, economic conditions that choked companies' abilities to finance equipment, and the difficulty of users adapting to sometimes painful readjustments in work processes. She notes that although electronic spreadsheets have made managers' jobs easier, packaged accounting software has been a boon to small companies, and electronic mail has increased the speed of communications, still, the paperless office is far from reality. In fact, because corporate executives have traditionally based their success on face-to-face interactions, such people are unlikely to make frequent use of impersonal computer notes.

Although American Hospital Supply has made its customers' switching decisions an uncomfortable choice by linking them to its corporate ordering system, most companies and vendors have an extremely difficult time making two computers talk to each other. In fact, lack of communications, poor documentation, incompatible peripherals, and scant adherence by vendors to software standards have caused executives to wonder why they should invest any more money in this tower of babble. Software exists to bridge these incompatibilities, but they are quite expensive and are usually supplied by small, unfamiliar "third-party" vendors.

Also, the human element was ignored. For example, security problems such as the highly publicized "hacker" break-ins at the Los Alamos nuclear facility, the Sloan-Kettering Cancer Institute, and TRW cause managers to wonder about the safety of their corporate data in electronic form. Blaming the technology without examining the weakest link—a dishonest or disgruntled employee—is all too common. Human issues probably are the reason for a mismatch of expectations and performance in artificial intelligence. For example, expert systems require an expert. The expert must be willing to analyze a lifetime of decision processes that have become second nature. They must be willing to give up the very information that makes them experts to a systems designer who typically knows little about their area of expertise. In return they get little more than thanks. Another reason for slow acceptance is self-interest. Managers and labor union members are well aware of factory automation's impact on jobs, the elimination of middle-management positions, and deskilling of clerical jobs. Skepticism and caution are human nature in such cases.

In most of these examples of skepticism and slowdown, the technology inherent in an adequate solution exists today. The tools exist to move U.S. corporations toward the factory of the future and a more efficient and effective workforce. However, it will take more than hardware dropped on the loading docks of the Fortune 500. It will require a realistic picture of technology's potential and its constraints. Also required is a commitment to work with a new innovation as a tool, not as a panacea.

The road to the automated workplace has been bumpy but, according to Salerno, "Despite the management challenges that computers pose, companies that have entered the electronic age have discovered advantages that they will never give up." In some organizations, computers are essential to daily operations; in others a distinct competitive advantage has arisen. Auto companies are not likely to give up their robots for human spot welders and paint sprayers. A bank without an automated teller machine (ATM) not only pays more for a human teller, but misses an opportunity to provide a convenient service that customers refuse to live without. The highly competitive airline industry could not exist, as we know it today, without interactive database access to customer and seat occupancy records. Likewise, customers are not likely to frequent a carrier that disregards the value of their time wasted while waiting in lines. (Just remember the last time you flew to a foreign country where airlines still kept records on chalkboards and handwritten customer lists. Shudder at the thought!) The cost of customer patronage cannot be measured in mere dollars; it has become a corporate survival issue that is determined by the use of technology.

It is time consultants, systems designers, and MIS managers join hands with executives and line managers to deliver results. We need to develop a technology strategy as a direct outgrowth of the corporate strategy. In some respects the computer industry slowdown will make vendors reassess their scruples and their approaches to customer satisfaction. At least it will allow the corporate decision maker breathing room to rationally choose a set of technologies that meets a real need.

NEW DEMANDS ON TECHNOLOGY

Contrary to the projections of many futurists, we are not, in a significant way, becoming a nation of electronic publishers, software developers, and telecommunications implementors. Although our economy has made drastic shifts where new jobs and entrepreneurial opportunities are developing, most of the technological advantages will be as a result of applying new methods in new ways to old problems. From this point of view, technology assessment is not new. Fredrick Taylor's "scientific management" laid the foundation for industrial engineering's time-and-motion studies in the early 1900s. Few people today would call this high-tech. But the objective of Taylor and the objectives of technology assessment as a discipline remain the same. Both seek to improve the age-old quest of technology—to match techniques and tools to meet human needs. This isn't hype, it's a fact of life. Humans have used tools to make life easier and make economic progress for hundreds of thousands of years. We just have more sophisticated tools to work with today. And since the pace of technical change is creating new tools faster than we can apply them, technology assessment is proposed, not as a new panacea, but as a rational (yet creative) approach to making sense of these new tools and their associated opportunities for competitive advantage in business.

As James Botkin and Dan Dimancescu of Harvard, and Ray Stata, president of Analog Devices, discuss in their book, *The Innovators*:

> Today's innovators are those who understand not only the new constraints affecting us but especially the new opportunities that beckon. . . . Computers and their associated electronics are not really "high technology" but "new technologies." . . . The real value of the so-called "high-tech" industries is as the new tool makers whose products can revitalize old industries.[7]

Information technologies involving computer-based systems are being asked to transcend established criteria for corporate contribution. The conventional notion of information systems is as a cost-displacement and productivity tool. That concept is being replaced with a more dynamic and exciting idea. Information is being realized in progressive companies as a business asset that is critical to the success of the organization. Winning and losing may be determined by the quality of decisions based on the corporate knowledge base. As a result, executives are paying as much attention to corporate data as they have traditionally paid to more tangible assets, such as manufacturing plants and equipment. Monitoring systems are being put in place, goals are being defined, and contribution to the bottom-line business results is expected. Smart managers are learning how to apply new technologies to improve existing processes and open up new possibilities. In addition, since the input to the corporate knowledge base comes from human beings, executives want to maximize the brain contribution of people and the creative content from those brains that go into making a total product or solution.[8]

Fundamentally, information technologies are moving from strictly supporting roles with cost containment as the primary benefit. As barriers for the competition, facilitators of customer or supplier dependency with high switching costs, and modifiers of the basis of competition, technology will be at the core of the firm's competitive survival.

COMPETITIVE DRIVERS

Creative application of information systems and associated computer and communications technologies is allowing companies to go beyond efficiency issues to seize clear advantages in the marketplace. The basis of competition is being restructured. Firms that competed on cost are finding that technology allows radically different features to be added to products, thus changing the cost-based competition to one of product differentiation. The reverse is also true. Companies that competed on differentiation are finding that, since a leading competitor has implemented a technology that neutralizes differentiation, cost is now more important. Let's take a look at some of the more common examples.

Consider the case of a large aerospace company that required its major suppliers to acquire computer-aided design (CAD) equipment to communicate directly with its CAD installation. The aerospace company saw dramatically reduced total cost, time of design changes, parts acquisition, and inventory. Because the aerospace company could now pick and choose among suppliers for the best prices, the suppliers saw a negation of the value of their product differences, with overall cost more important, according to Professor F. Warren McFarlan of Harvard.[9]

The basis of competition is also being changed in the area of specialized niche markets. In the financial services industry, insurance companies, banks, and brokerage houses are locked in fierce competition that is won or lost on the value-added features permitted by the use of information systems. A large financial services firm developed a sophisticated software product that allowed its sales force to prepare complex quotations on the customer's premises. This positioned the firm as an innovator in what had been a lackluster business. The sales force felt and looked more confident, and valuable time was gained to establish a firm market share.

A classic example, noted in business school cases and magazine articles, is the Merrill Lynch Cash Management Account. By combining information on a customer's checking, savings, credit card, and securities accounts into one consolidated database, idle funds are automatically moved into interest-bearing money market funds. Merrill Lynch pioneered this concept in 1978 and managed over $85 billion this way in 1985. Other banks eventually followed suit, but Merrill Lynch still has almost 70 percent of this market.[10]

Another example of value-added features due to technology is demonstrated by Aetna's Aeclaims system. By allowing customers access to their own group insurance claims, administrators of plans may do some analysis on their own to determine the effectiveness of in-house cost-containment efforts, for example. Similar systems by banks allow corporate treasurers to more actively manage cash in their firms' accounts.[11]

Citibank blanketed New York with automatic teller machines in the late 1970s. Using ATMs for more than cost-cutting teller replacements, Citibank was able to provide a customer convenience that more than doubled its demand deposit balances and almost tripled its market share from 5 percent to 13 percent.[12] ATMs are now a standard offering of most banks, and customers see them as a requirement, but over ten years ago Citibank sustained a definite competitive advantage over banks without extensive ATM networks and created a new requirement for entry to the market.

Marketing efforts are among the primary areas that can directly benefit from creative uses of technology. Another classic case heralded in the literature is American Airlines' use of electronic reservation systems to "lock in" travel agents. In the 1960s, American introduced the SABRE system to travel agents as a means to access the flight schedules, seating availability, and prices of all the major airlines. SABRE used display terminals not only to give flight information of American and its competitors, but also to influence the travel agent's purchase recommendation by listing American's flights first. Many agents never looked any further. As a result, American dramatically increased its market share and created total dependence by the agents on SABRE. By having access to its competitors' schedules and fares, American was also able to spot pricing opportunities and erode other carriers' shares of lucrative routes.

Ultimately the government insisted on an elimination of the bias in listing American flights; and other airlines, such as United, Eastern, Delta, and TWA developed their own systems. As the competition caught up, American was able to recognize an entirely new and profitable business—data processing. According to Catherine Harris of *Business Week*, SABRE is used by approximately 48 percent of the 24,000 automated travel agents in the United States. American Airlines pays $1.75 for every reservation booked on SABRE for other carriers, and American earned about $170 million before taxes on $338 million in revenues.[13]

American Hospital Supply's (AHS) use of distributed order entry terminals in customer sites is a well-known example of how rivals may be locked out of a market. AHS distributes a myriad of products from 8,500 manufacturers to over 100,000 hospitals and other health care providers.[14] By equipping its customers with electronic terminals linked to AHS's computer, hospitals enter orders themselves. Customers were "hooked." When introduced, the service was difficult to emulate by AHS's competitors, and customers refused devices from different vendors. AHS implemented a classic case of barriers to entry, as McFarlan notes.[15] In addition, AHS made it unattractive for its customers to easily switch to another distributor by using proprietary information systems and turnkey computers.

Information is the engine of competitiveness today. Managers in the packaged goods industry know this probably better than those in other industries. In a business where the margin on a bar of soap is measured in pennies (or fractions of a penny), high volume sales and low costs are the rule. Market share is paramount. Knowing this, Gerry Eskin and John Malec founded Information Resources, Inc. (IRI). By electronically tracking consumer behavior and correlating it to media exposure, IRI began providing consumer goods companies a measure of the effectiveness of their advertising dollars back in 1979. They turned small towns into market research laboratories. Universal Product Code (UPC) scanners in grocery stores tracked purchases, and a proprietary cable television system delivered test ads to individual households. The system, called Behavior-Scan, was more accurate than the largest service at that time (A.C. Nielsen's National Food Index) and cost up to 50 percent less, according to Wendy G. Rolm of *Infosystems*.[16] Ironically, the system was discussed with Nielsen before IRI was formed. Nielsen turned it down, and now IRI is one of their major competitors.

The increasing availability of marketing-oriented tools is of particular interest to chief executive officers (CEOs). Since marketing involves the continued growth of the revenue stream and since information technology is being used in creative ways to increase the revenue stream, block competitors, build customer loyalty, speed the time to market, and (of course) reduce costs, it comes as no surprise that competitive drivers are the drivers of technology.[17]

THE NEED FOR TECHNOLOGY ASSESSMENT

The competitive success of today's business clearly depends on the use of technology. Modern organizations face the dual challenge of keeping up with rapidly changing technology and making sense of it. Surpassing mere technology gatekeeping, managers must implement solutions to problems in a way that fundamentally changes HOW they do business and HOW customers relate to them. Gone are the days of merely automating operations. It comes as no surprise that executives find that automating bureaucracies creates efficient bureaucracies. The competitive application of technologies far surpasses simple automation. Companies with the edge are integrating technologies to increase their competitiveness. However, mere haphazard application of the latest technical bell or whistle provides little benefit.

A study by Patrick Marfisi of McKinsey & Company adds weight to this assertion.[18] In spite of the attempt by major computer vendors to control accounts by providing a "complete solution," Marfisi notes that "one stop shopping is a myth for leading edge customers with applications critical to their own competitiveness." The vendor strategy of comprehensive solutions is excellent for unsophisticated customers with applications that focus on efficiency—doing old procedures better. However, when a firm moves beyond simple automation of processes and administrative procedures to sophisticated applications that provide distinct competitive advantages, one-stop shopping can be a serious hindrance to achieving goals. Think about it. This is only common sense. Large computer vendors develop products for a mass market. Such products have mass appeal, identical hardware, inflexible software, and similar end-user interfaces. Mass products have the same relative payoff for every company that uses them. As a former product manager, I know that forecasts of sales are one of the most crucial factors in determining the features of a new computer product. Most vendors are forced to live with this reality.

Well, if a product can be purchased out of a catalog by you, it can also be purchased by all of your competitors. So when it comes to a distinct competitive advantage, companies are integrating various technologies (not just computers) from many vendors in a multidisciplinary fashion to solve their unique problems and, in the process, gain an advantage over the "also rans."

As an example, Marfisi notes how General Dynamics' goal of providing end-user access to all corporate data forced the aerospace and electronics giant to set up a joint research facility for its staff to work with IBM and AT&T. Neither vendor was either willing or able to deliver a system tailored to General Dynamics' needs, so forced integration was necessary. Likewise, Montgomery Ward's strategic retailing decision to move away from catalog centers in stores to customer call-in centers caused it to buy automatic call distributors from Rockwell while relying on its traditional sources for communications equipment.

Marfisi's examples underscore the trend in leading-edge companies: If the vendor won't do it, build your own expertise and integrate technologies.

This imperative will be seen more as stock brokers want improved access to market and customer data to improve their productivity and to do a better job of targeting accounts. Sales forces will continue to push the limits of remote system access to order entry, inventory, and delivery status records to improve customer satisfaction and by getting personally involved in the orders they have taken from key customers. Retailers and restaurateurs will drive systems integration with even more demands for corporate inventory management by linking up with point-of-sale terminals. The company with an advanced nibble of competitive advantage via new technologies will not settle for a suboptimal solution from "off-the-shelf" applications—no matter how big the vendor or how cozy the relationship. This is why technology assessment for unique systems design and integration is a growing concern.

The benefits of systems integration to suit corporate objectives are clear. What is less clear to many executives is the role of technology assessment. Questions we often hear are "Will it increase productivity?" and "Who in my organization is trained for such a task?" Let's discuss each point and its relevance to technology assessment.

In the words of Fred Toney, vice president of Cincinnati-based TechSoft Systems and close business associate of Strategic Systems, "Managers should avoid the common misconception that a causal relationship exists between actual productivity and technology."[19] Experts believe automation will increase productivity by at least 25 percent. Solow found, in factory studies back in 1957, that of the factors contributing to productivity increases, more than 80 percent were due to technology changes.[20] In spite of this, we should not believe that, as Toney notes, technology is a prescription for productivity. In the scramble for productivity by American business, we must take stock of the value of innovation. Some technologies provide direct productivity (i.e., efficiency improvements that help the firm accomplish structured tasks in less time and thus save tangible dollars). Other measures are less objective according to N. Dean Meyer.[21]

Technology assessment, since it ties into corporate goals and objectives, provides a structure for evaluating subjective technology decisions. When tangible productivity benefits are not clear cut, there are still times when technology investments should be made. These effectiveness benefits allow people to do a better job, do things that could not be done before, and potentially have an impact on the business process itself. Value-added benefits of effectiveness are typically where competitive advantages are realized, and they are clearly more significant in both size and relevance to the CEO's agenda than administrative efficiency. Technology cannot assure success in the form of either productivity or effectiveness, but it provides the means to do so.

Carleton Moten, senior consultant at Strategic Systems, describes technology assessment as a process that seeks to maximize the probability that such benefits are indeed realized. It also attempts to increase the positive impact an innovative development will have on the firm. Seen graphically in Figure 1-1, the SSI approach to technology assessment can widen a manager's scope of high-impact areas of the business that are ripe for technology. It can also broaden the range of high-impact technologies that can be applied to a specific domain of problems, as depicted in Figure 1-2. In either case, the SSI approach increases the probability of successful technology selection for a specific organizational scenario. We don't make this assertion because of some magical technique; we do so because the SSI process helps impose structure on what could otherwise be a shotgun approach. Successful project implementation is more probable because the projects selected affect the most crucial areas of the business and are more likely to elicit top management support.

Technology assessment involves a forward-looking approach to enhance competitiveness, productivity, and/or effectiveness opportunities. The champion of technology assessment in a firm needs to be an entrepreneurial individual. Expecting change, adapting to it, and seizing opportunities for the benefit of the organization is the rule, not the exception. Such a person must be willing to take risks, cut across functional lines, have a good sense of tactical and strategic plans, and understand the forces of the marketplace. As a collaborator with line managers, anticipation of business trends will be a valuable skill. The capability to evaluate innovations on their financial and human resource merits are as important as being able to judge products on their technical merits. As Sanjiv Sarin and Bennie Butts of North Carolina A&T propose, the technology assessment consultant "must not be linked only to successes and penalized for any failures . . . employees under such pressure will avoid any risks . . . and in the long run, will be detrimental to the survival of the organization."[22]

Technology assessment is merely a recommended method, not a scientific discipline. It requires knowledge of one's business, the environment, what competitors are up to, and what constraints the market and the government impose. It is a logical approach that requires analytical skills. Yet it dares one to be creative, intuitive, multidisciplinary, and make the most of the differences in one's staff. It has elements of an art blended with science and demands the practitioner to understand the maturity curves of products and technologies. Maturity curves, better known as *S-Curves*, help managers to understand whether they should invest in a new product or use it as a "cash cow." As noted by Richard Foster of McKinsey & Company, managers must

Figure 1-1
"Organization-Focused" Technology Assessment Program

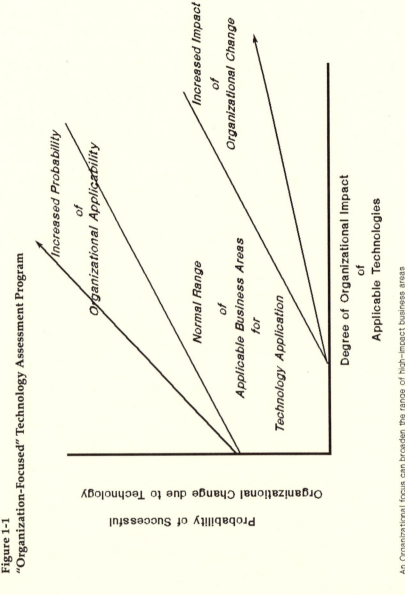

Increased Probability
of
Organizational Applicability

Normal Range
of
Applicable Business Areas
for
Technology Application

Increased Impact
of
Organizational Change

Degree of Organizational Impact
of
Applicable Technologies

Probability of Successful
Organizational Change due to Technology

An Organizational focus can broaden the range of high-impact business areas
where technology is applicable and increase the probability of success.

14

Figure 1-2
"Technology-Focused" Technology Assessment Program

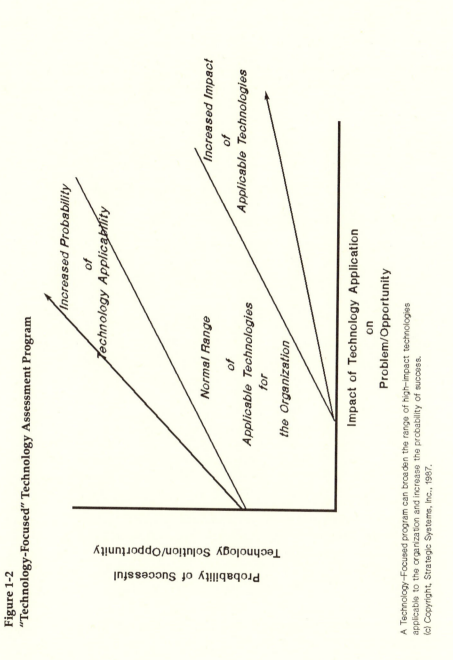

Increased Probability
of
Technology Applicability

Increased Impact
of
Applicable Technologies

Normal Range
of
Applicable Technologies
for
the Organization

Impact of Technology Application
on
Problem/Opportunity

Probability of Successful
Technology Solution/Opportunity

A Technology-Focused program can broaden the range of high-impact technologies
applicable to the organization and increase the probability of success.
(c) Copyright, Strategic Systems, Inc., 1987.

15

learn how to manage their businesses to take advantage of the discontinuities of economic cycles and of technology development cycles. In fact, according to Foster, these S-Curves give insight into technology developments
that allow a company to be the attacker, rather than the follower, in a particular industry.[23]

Technology for technology's sake is unacceptable in a competitive market. In
fact, it is likely to waste R&D resources and disrupt the human activities in
what is already a complex organization. Therefore, it makes sense that the
internal or external consultant who is assessing the potential impact of
emerging technologies on a business entity and its people:

1. Understand that corporate goals and objectives must be partners
   with the technology strategy.
2. Understand that science differs from technology, and this, in turn,
   helps focus the R&D strategy toward practical results.
3. Understand the trends and synergistic tendencies of the factors
   driving technology development.
4. Understand that successful technology assessment and organizational change require more than technology. Creative approaches
   by broadly skilled and motivated people complement the sterility
   of pure technology.

These are the primary points of this book.

HUMAN ISSUES FOR CONSIDERATION

Successful technology strategies require more than technology. This is the
basic message that I have carried with me throughout my career. Several
people have been instrumental in keeping this point on SSI's agenda but
none more personally significant than Margie Wells-Davis, a Cincinnati-
based socio-technical consultant. Over the past ten years, she has been the
driving force that helped us understand that technology assessment is hol-
low unless it takes a holistic approach, considering the management of business, organizational, and technology factors simultaneously.[24]

Modern organizations have come to understand that the achievement of
their goals requires proper attention to what is to be done (business objectives), how objectives can be met (the technological dynamic), and who will
do the work (its people). Since a change in either sphere of influence can
cause changes in others, Wells-Davis' *Total Effectiveness Model* (see Figure
1-3) stresses assessment of the factors influencing the external business

Figure 1-3
The Total Effectiveness Model

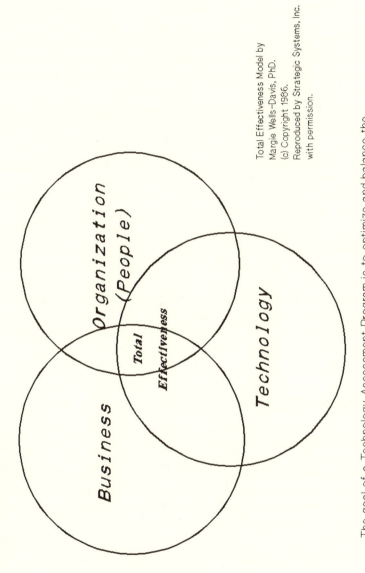

Organization
(People)

Total
Effectiveness

Business

Technology

The goal of a Technology Assessment Program is to optimize and balance the demands of business, the needs of people, and technology's opportunities.

environment, internal skill sets and organizational biases, and a technology's fit. In essence, the goal of an effective technology assessment process (indeed the challenge) is to optimize the selection and implementation of technologies and techniques in a way that balances the economic needs of the company and the human needs of its people.

Taking into account the human factors is imperative since people are the means to accomplishing the corporate objectives. This seems to be a particularly hard lesson to learn for engineers, consultants, and vendors. We continually see products that are virtually unusable. I have heard of several CEOs of computer companies—trained engineers who are renowned for their technical abilities and common sense—having difficulty assembling their home personal computers. These machines were built for Joe or Jane Average, true novices with little, if any, technical background. If trained engineers have trouble with relatively simple machines, it should come as no surprise that non-technical managers of mature industries are scared stiff of computers. By considering the human element, technology assessment has the capability of identifying such problems before a product selection is made and, at least, forewarning of training needs.

Other human issues are broader and somewhat philosophical, yet no less important to the overall process. If one wants to have an innovative organization in which there is indeed integration of new technologies for competitive advantage, then the corporate structure must foster innovation, value differences, promote interdisciplinary approaches across functional lines, and accept the inherent untidiness of the R&D process. Research cannot always be dealt with systematically. (This is the flip side of our criticism of engineers. Executives and line managers must also be tolerant of "technical people.") People don't get ideas in a systematic way. Ideas, especially creative technical ideas, are often the products of people with odd modes of thinking, who may not fit the "dress for success" mold, and who feel constrained with deadlines and accounting systems that track their time. Although reasonable guidance toward business goals is in order, creative ideas can be stifled by a bureaucracy.

Technical innovation, creativity, and utilization of human potential will require different approaches to old and new problems. Such approaches will need to build on the current educational process but also expand into uncharted waters for American industry. Intuition, multidisciplinary analyses, and asking questions in "offbeat" ways will accompany an expectation of lifelong learning to ward off technical obsolescence and to stay abreast of business trends. We recommend an approach to learning that stresses *learning how to learn* and *learning how to think*. Corporations will be asked to shoulder more and more of the educational burden. Also of importance, companies will continue to find that they must educate their employees as a matter of staying competitive.

American business must compete on the only clear margin it has left—the creativity of a diverse workforce and a constant stream of radical innovation. Shortsightedness and unreasonable suboptimization of administrative techniques cannot be allowed to dampen those creative juices. As Robert Frosch, former NASA administrator, states, "We cannot use a business attitude of the kind I can only describe as 'Let's compute the accounting results before we know what we are going to build.'"[25]

The organization itself must reassess its view of technological change. Since the major competitive advantages are likely to come from the exploitation of opportunities produced by change, change must be welcomed. Innovative thought will flourish in an organization that is self-adaptive to change. What are the characteristics of such organizations? According to Donald Davis of Old Dominion University:

> Organizations are likely to adopt innovations when they have strategies that stress technological advancement, structures that allow decentralized decision-making, limited formal rules and regulations, high proportions of managerial specialists who are professionally active, and managers who value new ideas and are receptive to change.[26]

There is a subtle side effect of the application of technologies to the business. Although scholarly debate rages as to the validity of the data, there is a common, though not scientific, belief that end-user computing such as spreadsheet applications (Lotus 1-2-3 and Visicalc, for example) and certainly some forms of computer programming may lead to improved thinking processes.[27] Using spreadsheets, managers not only reduce drudgery and plan more efficiently, they gain insight into the operations of their business. They are forced to think of relationships between variables and quantify them. Cause-and- effect, what-if kinds of simulations, and definition of parameters are valuable mental exercises for any manager. Likewise, managers who take a stab at writing their own programs have reported "improvements" in their ability to think logically and see relationships. We will not debate the scholars since these are subjective testimonials, but wouldn't it be of value to the organization to try any reasonable approach that improves the thinking of its managers?

When a technology assessment program is used to correlate innovation to (1) market opportunity, (2) corporate objectives, and (3) human potential, we have a situation where organizational success moves beyond marginal increases in productivity to a situation where successful companies "do right things right."[28]

NOTES

1. Michael E. Porter, *Competitive Advantage* (New York: The Free Press, 1985), p. 164.

2. "1986 Industry Outlook," *Business Week* (January 13, 1986).

3. John F. Rockart and Christine V. Bullen, *The Rise of Managerial Computing* (Homewood, Ill.: Dow Jones-Irwin, 1986), pp. vii-xx.

4. David H. Freedman, "Are We Expecting Too Much from Strategic IS?" *Infosystems* (January 1987), pp. 22-24.

5. Ibid.

6. Lynn M. Salerno, "What Happened to the Computer Revolution?" *Harvard Business Review* (November-December 1985), pp. 129-37.

7. James Botkin, Dan Dimancescu, and Ray Stata, *The Innovators: Rediscovering America's Creative Energy* (New York: Harper & Row, 1984), pp. 3, vii.

8. Donald A. Marchand and Forest W. Horton, *Infotrends: Profiting from Your Information Resources* (New York: John Wiley & Sons, 1986), pp. vii-26.

9. F. Warren McFarlan, "Information Technology Changes the Way You Compete," *Harvard Business Review* (May-June 1984), pp. 98-103.

10. Catherine L. Harris, "Information Power: How Companies are Using New Technologies to Gain a Competitive Edge," *Business Week* (October 14, 1985), p. 109.

11. Ibid., p. 111.

12. Ibid.

13. Ibid., p. 109.

14. Ibid.

15. McFarlan, "Information Technology Changes the Way You Compete," p. 99.

16. Wendy G. Rolm, "A Capital Idea," *Infosystems* (November 1986), pp. 48-52.

17. David H. Freedman, "The CEO & MIS: A Promising Partnership," *Infosystems* (February 1986), pp. 28-30.

18. Patrick Marfisi, "The Myth of One-Stop Shopping," *Business Computer Systems* (June 1986), pp. 37-44.

19. Frederick Toney, "Will Microcomputer Automation Increase Productivity?" *Tidbits* (TechSoft Systems, Vol. 1, 1985).

20. R. Solow, "Technical Change and the Aggregate Production Function," *Review of Economics and Statistics* (1957), pp. 312-30.

21. N. Dean Meyer, "Efficiency vs. Effectiveness," *SIGOIS Bulletin* (Association for Computing Machinery, Winter, 1987), pp. 7-8.

22. Sanjiv S. Sarin and Bennie Butts, "The Industrial Engineer as Entrepreneurial Individual for Managing Change," *Industrial Engineering* (Institute of Industrial Engineers, July 1986), pp. 16-19.

23. Richard N. Foster, *Innovation: The Attacker's Advantage* (New York: Summit Books, 1986), pp. 31-105.

24. Margie E. Wells-Davis, discussions during December 1986, Cincinnati.

25. Robert A. Frosch, "R&D Choices and Technology Transfer," *Research Management* (May-June 1984), pp. 11-14.

26. Donald D. Davis, "Technological Innovation and Organizational Change," *Managing Technological Innovation: Organizational Strategies for Implementing Advanced Manufacturing Technologies* (San Francisco: Jossey-Bass, 1986), pp. 1-18.

27. R.E. Mayer, J.L. Dyck, and W. Vilberg, Learning to Program and Learning to Think: What's the Connection? *Communications of the ACM* (Association for Computing Machinery, July 1986), pp. 605-610.

28. Industry slogan popularly attributed to W. Edwards Deming.

2

Technology vs. Science

THE ESSENCE OF SCIENCE AND TECHNOLOGY

This book deals extensively with technology as it relates to business problems and opportunities. But just what do we mean by *technology* or, for that matter, *science*? Numerous definitions and descriptions of these words have been written, none of which have been able to succinctly encompass all of the characteristics of these terms. The "man in the street," according to J.B. Conant, considers science to be the activity of people who work in laboratories and whose discoveries have made possible modern industry and medicine.[1]

This statement, although it may appear to be true to many lay persons, is quite shallow as a meaningful description of what science is. For example, many people who clearly qualify as scientists do not have any association with laboratories, and their discoveries do not have any direct applicability in either modern industry or medicine. As important as contributions to these areas have been, this concept illustrates the need to develop working definitions with significant key words so we may clarify just what concepts science and technology employ.

Science is the body of knowledge obtained by methods of observation. It is derived from the Latin word *scientia*, which simply means knowledge, and the German word *wisenschaft*, which means systematic, organized knowledge. Thus, science, to the extent that it is equivalent to *wisenschaft*, consists not of isolated bits of knowledge, but only of that knowledge that has been systematically assembled and put together in some sort of organized manner.[2] In particular, the science with which we are concerned is a body of knowledge which derives its facts from observations, connects these facts with theories, and then tests or modifies these theories as they succeed or fail in predicting or explaining new observations. In this sense, science has a relatively recent history—perhaps four centuries.[3]

Although, science as an activity has existed as long as humans have existed, the modern Western notion of science began with the European awakening during the High Middle Ages, the Renaissance, and the Industrial Revolution. Therefore we should clearly recognize that science, as America understands it, is a European concept that describes the process for gathering data about nature, using that data to draw general conclusions, and testing the conclusions under critical observation. Make no mistake as to the thrust here—the process is important in the European concept of science. This should not block our interest in broadening that concept to include definitions from other cultures, personal definitions, or that of the ancients. However, we must recognize that the critical difference between the modern view of science and the ancient view rests on the methods employed and the ultimate aims for using scientific knowledge. More will be said about the alternative views of science shortly; for now, let us develop an understanding of the term *technology*.

Much of the relevance of science to mankind and to society arises by way of technology. There are intimate relationships between science and technology, yet science is not technology and technology is not science. The origin of the word *technology* gives valuable insight into its meaning. It is derived from the Greek words *techne* and *logos*. The former meaning art or craft, and the latter signifying discourse or organized words. The practice of technology frequently is that of an art or craft, as distinguished from science which is precise and is based on established theoretical considerations. Even though we do not normally think of technology as consisting of written or spoken words, as implied by *logos*, technology does involve the systematic organization of processes, techniques, and goals. Technology is applied, but not necessarily based on science. In fact, as California State University's Robert Fischer notes, "To define technology as applied science is to miss much of the significance of the relationship that exists between science and technology."[4] He defines technology as the totality of the means employed by peoples to provide material objects for human sustenance and comfort.

One connotation of the working definition of technology is that it is a human activity. It is people who use the products of technology. Furthermore, it is people whose livelihood and comfort is the goal of technology, whether this goal is actually accomplished by technology or not.

According to Fischer, technology is directed in specific instances toward specific material objects—that is, toward the production of physical objects. This is not to exclude the importance of non-material concepts to human sustenance and comfort, but it is meant to drive home the central theme that technology is driven by physical needs. By definition, technology is not neutral because it is directed toward satisfying a physical need, as determined by a human value system. Technology is power, and one who controls technology controls the power inherent in its application. Technology is defined, to some degree, by our relationship with the environment. It involves our attempt to control and shape the world and to make use of whatever resources are available in that environment.[5]

The basic Western motive for "bringing about technology" is the desire to obtain more or better material things. There are of course more immediate and less profound motivations for individuals in either science or technology (such as the desire to get a paycheck and retain one's job), as Fischer notes. Other points of comparison involve grander motives, such as the ancient beliefs of using technology to devote monuments to gods, heroes, or esthetics. The concept of technology as "more and better material things" is a Western concept born out of the flowering of knowledge and materialism that was the European Renaissance.

Technology has a much longer history than science—a history as long as humanity. We have evolved together with our tools and techniques over millions of years. The major changes in human population are due to the technology we have developed to domesticate grain, irrigate land, and store and preserve food. We exist by the generosity of the earth, but how many of us live and how many of us starve depends on how well we use and distribute the earth's resources. During the pre-European period of the Inca, Aztec, and Mayan civilizations, perhaps 15 million people lived in the Americas. Most lived in the major civilizations with cities in Mexico and Central and South America where agriculture was relatively advanced. Most human labor was used to obtain food. We now have well over a half billion people in the Americas with less than 5 percent of our labor force needed to produce food.[6] Without technical developments in agriculture, we could not sustain such a population growth, and in no way would we have the time or the physical energy to develop a more advanced civilization. All of our time and effort would be devoted to the maintenance of life.

Technology has developed separately from science throughout most of recorded history. Technological change has generally derived empirically, simply by trial and error. The method used in proceeding to the development of new technological advances is determined primarily on the basis of two factors: (1) the existing technology, and (2) the existing scientific knowledge. This scientific knowledge used in technology is not a replacement for the trial-and-error method of technology; rather, it provides a means of selecting what trial to undertake next and thus contributes to the efficiency and effectiveness of the trial-and-error process. Technology can use scientific knowledge and, in this sense, can be sometimes viewed as applied science. Yet much technology continues to be developed with little or no basic scientific knowledge. For example, Fischer cites how photography was developed to a high degree even though many of its early practitioners had little understanding of the underlying chemical phenomena.[7]

For our use, let us say that technology is science plus purpose. While science is the study of the nature around us and subsequent development of scientific "laws," technology is the practical application of those laws, in sometimes non-rigorous ways, toward the achievement of some purpose—usually material.[8]

HISTORICAL PERSPECTIVE

As previously mentioned, our conception of science and technology has a relatively modern European flair. However, make no mistake about it, both science and technology existed with different underlying assumptions before the Renaissance, before the Roman Empire, before the Greeks conquered the "known world," and even before the great flowering of Egypt. Both concepts and their applications may be traced directly to the "cradle of civilization." As noted by historian Chancellor Williams, ancient cultures that occupied the fertile crescent of the Nile valley prior to Egypt's greatness were the exclusive province of Kushites, Nubians, Shebans, Mesopotamians, and Thebans, which we now refer to collectively as Ethiopians.[9] These ancient people were accomplished agriculturalists and were very religious. Indeed, religion to the Ethiopians was far more than ritual reflecting beliefs. It was a reality reflected in their way of life. Religion from the earliest times became the dynamic force in the development of all the major aspects of their civilization.

Their belief in immortality was a simple matter of course and beyond the realm of debate. This belief was the great inspiration for ancient technology. The Ethiopians built, on a grand scale, structures that were meant to stand forever. Actually, it was necessity that gave birth to mathematics and astronomy. Building the Ethiopian pyramids and the most elaborate system of temples the world had known required the development of engineering.[10]

Therefore, we see that Ethiopian scientific and technical development was driven by religious beliefs. This contrasts to the modern Western view of technology which is embedded with drivers for a more-and-better world. Both schools of thought stress the products of technology, but the motivations are quite different.

Many of the ancient temples were dedicated to reflective thinking and discovery—what we might call colleges. These temple-centered colleges fostered free discourse and viewed science as purely a process of thought. Scholars from foreign lands came to study, and from here religious ideas and their architectural designs spread abroad. Since the Ethiopian empire at that time included what we now call ancient Egypt, it was natural that these facets of the Upper Nile culture should spread to the lower Nile and the northernmost part of the continent. The early Greeks were heavily influenced by these same architectural structures, scientific methods, and religious concepts, according to Williams. The Greeks eagerly copied, reshaped, and made them into parts of a new Western culture.[11]

The Ionian Greeks exemplified by Thales of Miletus, Anaximander, Pythagoras, Socrates, and Plato developed many of their ideas using ancient Ethiopian and Egyptian works as their base. The Ionian Greeks had an earthy tradition that stressed the enjoyment of life, commercial property, esthetic refinement, and acceptance of newcomers—all of which allowed free thought and inquiry to flourish. From its earliest manifestations, the Greek mind had turned to natural philosophy (at least the minds of the upper classes). The beginnings of Greek philosophical thought were identical with the beginnings of Greek science. Led by Thales of Miletus, the Greeks saw the formation of the earth by natural processes, no longer through an act of the gods. Greek science by the sheer process of speculation, argument, intuition, plus an occasional dash of empirical reasoning had moved within the space of two generations from the early mythical notions to a point that is surprisingly close to modern concepts.[12]

"The Ionians conceived of nature as a completely self motivating entity," explains science historian Thomas Goldstein. The workings of the universe occurred as mere extensions of the primordial chaos, automatic functions of its basic elements. Matter possessed its own evolutionary quality. "Order" and "law" were mere concepts superimposed by the human mind on the autonomous processes of nature. Nature knew of no laws. Pythagoras is credited with introducing the vision of an intrinsic natural order, and Plato adopted this vision.[13]

Aristotle, Plato's pupil, took his master's basic philosophy, added more structure, and advocated verification of intuitive natural laws with objective observation. Like Plato, Aristotle thought it necessary to, first of all, understand and explain the workings of the human mind and to show what kinds of reasoning were valid and could be relied on to provide knowledge with surety. In his *Organon* or *Logic*, Aristotle made clear the processes of logical, reasoned thinking for proving the correctness of its conclusions. He made plain the steps by which a science or body of knowledge may be firmly built from its starting point in certain fundamental axioms or obvious statements, perceived intuitively to be true. Every science, as Aristotle pointed out, must begin with a few general truths. They cannot be logically proved, but our minds by simple intuition accept them as obviously true. Without such assumptions as foundations, we could never start to build anything.[14]

Louise Loomis, editor of a modern translation of Aristotle's scientific philosophies, notes that Aristotle reasoned like Plato, from ideal abstract principles, whenever the subject of the reasoning lay outside the field of observation possible to him. However, he was also willing to reject or change his theories when a closer examination of nature proved them wrong. Both a great thinker and a great scientist, Aristotle set the tone for future scientists by his method of inquiry and an avowed determination to yield to observation as the final arbiter. As a result, an atmosphere of sober empiricism distinguished the Hellenic Greeks from the Ionians, with Aristotle credited as being a great dividing line in Greek history. Having channeled the power of Greek philosophical thought into a logical system of scientific classification, Aristotle's system came to exercise an enormous influence over European science for the next 2,000 years.[15]

The classic Roman civilization built upon Greek science to develop their mighty empire with its renowned technical prowess. The Romans, being driven by conquest, glory, commerce, and an increasing need to find new resources, never really flowered as scientists. Free thought was not the hallmark of Rome. The Roman way of doing things was impressed on its citizens and conquered states as a matter of standard procedure. The Romans did, however, undertake massive engineering feats such as extended roads, aqueducts, and highly structured cities.[16] Here technology flourished, but no new ideas of "earth-shattering" philosophical importance stand out. Great translators of other works, the Romans were exploiters of resources and fantastic implementors of technology.

As Rome crumbled under the weight of countless invasions, the cosmic vision of the Greeks and the technological achievements of the Romans shriveled. With Europe overrun by the Germanic tribes, scientific inquiry was stunted for a millennium. Europe slept in a stupor of ignorance for 1,000 years. "To those who lived through the catastrophe, it seemed that the utter breakdown of civilization had come, the ruin of everything humanity had ever tried to create over thousands of years, a verdict from a wrathful heaven," according to Goldstein.[17] Europeans reacted with a radical readjustment of mind, turning their backs on the world of the senses which now seemed unworthy of intellectual scrutiny. For them, the end of Roman civilization meant a steadfast attachment to the dogma of Christianity. To Europeans it offered the only hope left.

Medieval Christianity stunted the growth of science but not that of technology. Since it asked, indeed demanded, renunciation of the world of the senses, Christianity left no room for scientific observation. However, in an ironic way it fostered the development of ever-powerful weaponry to carry out its Holy War against the Moslems. The development of armor, hardened weapons, better cavalry equipment, battering rams, catapults, fortresses, and cannons all contributed to the steady growth of European technology. Over time, an influx of resources, increased improvements in agriculture under the feudal system, a burgeoning economic prosperity, and exposure to very diverse cultures as a result of the Crusades made it difficult to reconcile reality with the world-denying traditions of the medieval mind.

When the hope given by the church was no longer needed, new morals and money provided the impetus for Europeans to cast the church aside in favor of a new age—the Renaissance. Suddenly, being earthy and gauche was in. Once again Europe entered an age of free inquiry, but this time a novel twist accompanied the new age.

The twist was represented by a view of life advocated by a new breed of wealthy philosopher/scientist. The European scientific revolution of the sixteenth and seventeenth centuries began with Nicolaus Copernicus who overthrew the geocentric view of Ptolemy and the Bible that had been accepted for over a thousand years. After Copernicus, the earth was no longer thought to be the center of the universe but merely one of the many planets that circled a minor star in an insignificant galaxy. Radical in its impact, this view of the world robbed humans of their proud position in the center of God's creation. (Actually, a Greco-Egyptian named Aristarchus developed the same theory 2,000 years earlier.[18])

Without dogmatic theological constraints, other scientists such as Johannes Kepler who is credited with the laws of planetary motion, Galileo Galilei the rediscoverer of many of the principles of gravitation and the inventor of the telescope, and Sir Isaac Newton who combined much of his previous work into the laws of motion each contributed to the Renaissance's spirit of inquiry.

Two aspects of these scientists' work stand as foundations of modern science: (1) the empirical approach based on objective, rational observation, and (2) their use of mathematics to describe nature. These principles laid the groundwork for modern scientific methods of inquiry and were forcefully argued by René Descartes, the philosopher, and Francis Bacon, the theologian.[19] Therefore, Europe awakened to an approach to knowledge that goes back through the works of Bacon, Newton, Copernicus, and Aristotle, and that included the processes of observation, generalization, explanation, and prediction fully rooted in an earthy materialism, indicative of the age. This view of knowledge became pervasive—changing assumptions not only in science but in the entire social fabric of Europe.

Europe came to understand that

1. Nature (the physical realm) is real,
2. Nature is orderly, and
3. Nature is, in part, understandable.

To what extent can we actually know nature? Carl Sagan eloquently expresses our potential and limitations as he compares our physical realm to the world of a grain of salt. He discusses, in *Broca's Brain*, that the 1,000 trillion sodium and chlorine atoms in a grain of salt would overwhelm our ability to understand salt if we were forced to know about every atom. This is because the human brain has a limit of approximately 10 trillion neurons and dendrites (connections between neurons). Since there are more atoms in salt than connections in our brains, we can never expect to know everything with certainty in the microscopic world of a grain of salt. Just as unknowable are phenomena on the cosmic scale of the universe.[20]

If we use the empirical approach, however, and seek regularities and principles, we can understand both the grain of salt and the universe through extrapolation. We may never understand everything, but we can get some good indications that allow us to draw rational conclusions.

Sagan's main point is that our scientific method of inquiry is based on our senses. Because we inhabit physical space and time, phenomena outside this realm—the microscopic world of the interior of atoms or the macroscopic world of the universe—are beyond our physical senses. Although we may use electron microscopes to probe the atom or radio telescopes to study the universe, we cannot escape the fact that these are merely devices which transform signals into the forms that our senses can recognize. Therefore, if we understand our limitations, we will be forced to understand the limitations of science.

This is an important lesson for a culture that depends heavily on science and technology. We have become quite adept at conquering tangibles with technology. From medical science to space travel, from instantaneous communications to automated warfare, Western science and technology have consistently proven their utility. When we turn to the world of the intangibles, technology and science face definite limitations. Social problems transcend mathematical descriptions and involve emotions that cannot be touched, measured, or successfully manipulated. Theological questions transcend our three physical dimensions of space and our one dimension of time. What exists beyond those dimensions can only be entertained as speculation or believed through blind faith. Science is a search for truth, and truth is limited to the facts of nature that are there for observation via our senses. As a result, technology cannot emulate human feelings, and science cannot define God.

THE R&D STRATEGY

As we have seen, science has many facets. In essence, it is pure neutral knowledge extracted painfully from nature through systematic means for dissemination to all humanity. Technology is not science. Technology is how we do things, not how we think of them. However, technology relies very heavily on basic scientific knowledge in addition to existing technologies.

There is also a strong influence in the reverse direction. Modern science relies to a large extent on current technology as well as on prior scientific knowledge. Science and technology reinforce each other by complex interactions. Each one, science or technology, can build upon itself or upon a linkage from one to the other. Technology is dependent on science for knowledge of the properties of materials and energy and for predicting the behavior of natural forces. "Science is equally dependent upon technology for its tools and instruments, for preparation of materials, for the storage and dissemination of information, and for the stimulation of further research," according to Fischer.[21]

Indeed, science is not technology and technology is not science, but they are firmly interrelated. One could not exist in modern society without the other. Although science and technology are closely related, a competitive organization needs to clearly delineate the components of its research and development (R&D) strategy. If we loosely correlate science with the research part of R&D and technology with the development part, then a firm needs to know whether there is too much of a tilt toward science or technology. A company should determine whether excessive emphasis is placed on "blue-sky" theory without practical results or, conversely, whether the firm is ignoring important new developments in basic research in favor of a purely pragmatic, short-term, tangible-return development focus. Overweighting either end of the R&D continuum can be a prescription for long-term stagnation.

We have found that research centers, think tanks, laboratories, high-tech manufacturers, and other organizations whose products are, in essence, "technologies" need strong scientific research programs as input to their technology product development strategies. However, companies producing goods and services (i.e., those whose products are other than technologies), need to consider concentrating on technology strategies as input to their product value chains, as a means to improve processes and as a way to focus limited R&D funds. Finding just the right balance between science and technology in the R&D strategy is the first step toward ensuring a successful technology assessment effort.

NOTES

1. J.B. Conant, *Science and Common Sense* (New Haven: Yale University Press, 1951).

2. Robert Fischer, *Science, Man & Society* (Philadelphia: W.B. Sanders, 1975), pp. 5-7.

3. Joseph B. Platt, "The Value of Science and Technology to Human Welfare," *Bulletin of the Atomic Scientists* (October 1973).

4. Fischer, *Science, Man & Society*, p. 76.

5. Ibid.

6. Platt, "The Value of Science and Technology to Human Welfare."

7. Fischer, *Science, Man & Society*, p. 77.

8. Richard C. Dorf, *Technology, Society, and Man* (San Francisco: Boyd & Fraser, 1974), p. 1.

9. Chancellor Williams, *The Destruction of Black Civilization* (Dubuque, Iowa: Kendall/Hunt, 1971), pp. 34-35.

10. Williams, *The Destruction of Black Civilization*, p. 35.

11. Ibid.

12. Thomas Goldstein, *The Dawn of Modern Science* (Boston: Houghton-Mifflin, 1980), pp. 48-64.

13. Ibid., p. 52.

14. Louise R. Loomis, ed., *Aristotle, On Man and the Universe* (Roslyn, N.Y.: Walter J. Black, 1971), pp. xi-xxxviii.

15. Ibid.

16. L. Sprague DeCamp, *The Ancient Engineers* (New York: Ballentine Books, 1976), pp. 172-280.

17. Goldstein, *The Dawn of Modern Science*, p. 55.

18. Carl Sagan, *Cosmos* (New York: Random House, 1980), pp. 14-21.

19. Fritjof Capra, *The Turning Point* (New York: Simon & Schuster, 1982), pp. 15-120.

20. Carl Sagan, *Broca's Brain* (New York: Random House, 1974), pp. 15-16.

21. Fischer, *Science, Man & Society*, p. 78.

3

Technological Change

SCIENTIFIC PARADIGM SHIFTS

Every individual lives and acts in accordance with his or her own worldview. A wide variety of views have been formulated and adhered to by people. Some are limited in scope; others are more comprehensive. Some have been well thought out and developed with precision; others are vague and ill-defined. Some are based on reason, others on emotion, and most on some combination of both.[1]

Cultural development has been facilitated by evolving, sometimes revolutionary, paradigms. The worldviews held by individuals or by groups are very influential in determining behavior as well as in determining motivations, attitudes, and actions.

Scientists and engineers, being fully human, also experience the effects of paradigms. They and their findings are influenced by the mainstream of social thought framed by current technology and prevalent belief systems.

By using knowledge of the universe, creativity, and a scientific approach to problem solving, scientists develop new paradigms. What actually causes them to change views as new evidence suggests a revision of a school of thought was thoroughly examined by MIT professor, Thomas Kuhn, a science historian and philosopher, in his landmark book, *The Structure of Scientific Revolutions.*[2]

Kuhn described a paradigm as a way of seeing the world and practicing science in it. The characteristics of a paradigm include new scientific achievements sufficiently unprecedented to attract an enduring group of adherents away from competing modes of scientific activity and, at the same time, sufficiently open-ended to leave all sorts of problems for the new group of practitioners to solve. Kuhn notes that paradigm development goes through several predictable structural stages from "normal science" to new paradigm acceptance.[3]

Normal science as defined by Kuhn means the body of research firmly based on one or more past scientific achievements that some particular scientific community acknowledges for a time as supplying the foundation for its further practice.[4] Today such achievements are the basic recounts, though seldom in their original form, by elementary and advanced textbooks. The findings of such achievements are the bases for all underlying scientific assumptions, which free the scientific community from constantly reexamining its first principles. This freedom allows members of that community to concentrate exclusively upon the subtlest and most esoteric of the phenomena that concern it. Inevitably this increases the effectiveness and efficiency with which the group as a whole solves new problems.

There are always competing schools of thought, each of which constantly questions the very foundations of the others. It is these competing schools that provide science with a self-correcting mechanism that ensures that the foundations of normal science will not go unchallenged.[5]

Scientific revolutions are inaugurated by a growing sense, often restricted to a narrow subdivision of creative minorities within the scientific community, that an existing paradigm has ceased to function adequately in the explanation of an aspect of nature for which that paradigm itself had previously led the way. This sense of crisis drives a reevaluation of the existing view and need not be generated by the work of the community that experiences the crisis. For instance, new instruments such as the electron microscope or new laws like Maxwell's wave theories may develop in one specialty, and their assimilation may create a crisis in another.

So as the crisis, that common awareness that something has gone wrong, shakes the very foundations of established thought, it generates a scientific revolution. Just as in politics, scientific revolutions seem revolutionary only to those whose paradigms are affected by them. To outsiders they may seem normal parts of the developmental process, almost invisible. Astronomers, for example, could accept X-rays as a mere addition to knowledge since their paradigms were unaffected by the existence of the new radiation. But for the Kelvins, Crookeses and Roentgens, whose research dealt with radiation theory and cathode ray tubes, the emergence of X-rays necessarily violated one paradigm as it created another. From their perspective, these rays could only have been discovered by something going wrong with normal science.

Those scientists whose paradigms are threatened typically react with resistance. When the number of instances that refute the old paradigm grows beyond supportable structures of the establishment, only then does a new paradigm arise. The decision to reject a paradigm is always simultaneously a decision to accept another with the judgment leading to that decision involving the comparison of both paradigms with nature and with each other.

Kuhn explains that revolutions close with a total victory for one of two opposing camps, with the winner rewriting scientific knowledge. Will the victorious group ever say that the result of its victory has been something less than progress? That would be admitting that they are wrong and the old paradigm holders are right. To the victors, the outcome of a revolution must be defined as progress, and they are uniquely positioned to make certain that future members of their community see past history in the same way because the new paradigm holders are the ones who get their work published.[6]

When a new paradigm repudiates a past one, a scientific community simultaneously renounces the past paradigm's experiments and subsequent textbooks. Scientific education makes use of no equivalent of the art museum or the library of classics, according to Kuhn. The result is sometimes a drastic distortion in the scientists' perception of their discipline's past. More than the practitioners of other creative fields, the scientist comes to see his or her discipline as evolving in a straight line to the present paradigm. In essence, the new paradigm is seen as progress, thus no alternative is available to the scientist while remaining in the field. The new paradigm is free to mature until the endless circle of challenge and debate inevitably signals its death.

Kuhn continues by challenging those who claim that when paradigms change, the world itself changes. Rather, led by a new paradigm, scientists actually adopt new instruments and look in new places. Even more important, scientists see new and different things when looking with familiar instruments in places they have looked before. It is almost as if the professional community had been suddenly transported to another planet where familiar objects are seen in a different light and are joined by unfamiliar ones as well. Of course, there is no geographical transplantation. Outside the laboratory, life continues as before. But paradigm shifts cause scientists to see the world differently, and they, in effect, are responding to a different world. It then becomes only a matter of time before their paradigms become popularized in a community of technologists and the social fabric begins to be rewoven as a result.

TECHNOLOGICAL DRIVERS

Technological change occurs as a result of economic or social necessity. It may occasionally be the result of rational debate between competing schools, but it is more likely to be driven by a combination of external forces, and, as noted earlier, technology frequently is the product of creative attempts to solve a problem. Such creativity may involve trial and error and a flash of intuition (i.e., insight).

Insight—the "aha" of problem solving—influences science but drives technology. When combined with a goal, insight allows us to apply scientific findings in new ways to attack old problems of physical survival, comfort, and convenience. Technologists, in the form of inventors and engineers, also experience revolutions of thought but in a very different environment than scientists. Technologists hardly, if ever, invent without help from colleagues and predecessors. Unlike science, technology seldom throws out old paradigms; it builds on them. Vertical progress comes from constantly improving old technologies, and spin-offs result from horizontal exchange of ideas across disciplinary boundaries.

Progress, of course, is relative to the goals of technology, the inventor, and those people who are affected by the new development. For example, during the introduction of robots into the American auto industry, few line workers considered them progress; however, engineers and managers viewed them as a triumph toward bottom-line corporate goals. Technology, being goal directed, relies on relative definitions to define progress. Despite this relativism of perspectives, technological progress can and does occur in vertical and horizontal directions by integrating sciences, innovative techniques, and old technologies. In reality, technical progress follows the parameters described by futurist John Naisbitt: "Change occurs when there is a confluence of both changing values and economic necessity, not before."[7]

Economics and human goals are the drivers of technological innovation. A good summary of the ways in which technologists experience the effects of economics and human values was presented by BBC reporter and author of *Connections*, James Burke. Burke designates six major initiators of technical innovation. They are deliberate invention, accidents, spin-offs, war, religion, and the environment.[8]

First, as one might expect, technical innovation occurs as a result of deliberate attempts to develop it. When inventors like Lewis Howard Latimer and Thomas Edison began work on the incandescent bulb, it was done in response to the inadequacy of the arc light. All the means were available: a vacuum pump to evacuate the bulb, electric current, the filament which the arc light used, and carbon for the filament. With these components, the remainder of the required work was the synthesis of technologies toward a definite goal—the light bulb's creation.

A second event that frequently occurs is that an attempt to find one thing leads to the discovery of another. For example, William Perkin, searching for an artificial form of quinine, used some of the molecular combinations available in coal tar and accidentally found that the black sludge produced by one of his experiments turned out to be the first artificial aniline dye.

Unrelated developments have decisive effects on the primary event. An example of such spin-off developments can be seen by the development of paper. The medieval textile revolution, which was based on the use of the spinning wheel and the horizontal loom, lowered the price of linen to the point where enough of it became available in rag form to revolutionize the paper industry. Other examples of how unforeseen circumstances play a leading role in technical innovation are discussed by Burke. This includes the stimulation of mining activities for metals to make cannons when Chinese gunpowder was exported to Europe and the development of a barometer as a result of frequent flooding of mines and the failure of pumps.

The fourth and fifth factors are all too familiar: war and religion. The need to find more effective means of defense (or offense) has driven technology from the most ancient of times. The use of the cannon led to defensive architectural developments which made use of astronomical instruments. As previously discussed, ancient Ethiopian, Egyptian, and pre-European indigenous American (Inca, Aztec, and Mayan) religious beliefs led to great strides in engineering and architecture, and the Islamic world developed advanced astronomy because of the need to pray, feast, and fast at specific times.

Finally, physical and climatic conditions play important roles. For example, the extreme changes in Europe's winters in the twelfth and thirteenth centuries provided urgent need for more efficient heating. The chimney filled the need and had a profound effect on the cultural life of that continent.

For whatever reasons we seek to apply, technology borrowing from scientific revolutions forces changes in thought as does science, but it goes beyond science by modifying behavior. For example, because of the social effects sometimes wreaked upon the organization by technological change, such advances are frequently resisted by paradigm holders unable to see the need for change. However, one fact remains certain: American industry cannot turn its backs on technical change as the English Luddites tried when they destroyed their textile looms. Technology will not go away that easily, and the company that ignores innovation tends to meet it again under more unfriendly circumstances—for example, as an ally of the competition.

A wiser approach is to assist, rather than fight, the technical change process. This is especially important in light of an examination of the history of successful new companies. As a later discussion of technology trends and maturity curves will show, phenomenal growth of creative new firms frequently results from exploiting technical change instead of shying away from it. In today's competitive environment, organizations really have no choice in the long run. They must embrace technical change! It was best summarized by Francis Bacon in his essay "Of Innovations":

> Retention of custom is as turbulent a thing as an innovation; and they that reverence too much old times are but a scorn to the new. . . . Surely every medicine is an innovation and he that will not apply new remedies must expect new evils.[9]

NOTES

1. Fischer, *Science, Man & Society*, pp. 3-173.

2. Thomas S. Kuhn, *The Structure of Scientific Revolutions* (Chicago: University of Chicago Press, 1970), pp. 1-181.

3. Ibid.

4. Ibid., p. 10.

5. Ibid., p. 163.

6. Ibid., p. 166.

7. John Naisbitt and Patricia Aburdene, *Re-inventing the Corporation* (New York: Warner Books, 1985), p. 42.

8. James Burke, *Connections* (Boston: Little, Brown, 1978), pp. 289-95.

9. Francis Bacon, *The Essays or Councils, Civil and Moral: of Francis Ld. Verulam* (Mount Vernon, N.Y.: Peter Pauper Press), pp. 96-97.

4

Technology Assessment Considerations

If the only tool you have is a hammer,
you tend to see every problem as a nail.
—Abraham Maslow

Change is a certainty in business today. Managers have to plan and adapt to economic change and competitive pressures. In this environment, great strides have been made in reducing costs through automation of highly structured tasks, but it is increasingly difficult to gain and sustain a competitive advantage. At the same time, regulatory and organizational pressures make it more difficult to manage capital assets, personnel, information resources, and unstructured decision-making processes.

To survive and prosper, businesses have to make these assets more productive. The challenge goes beyond making isolated productivity gains; the organization as a whole must be managed as a resource. This is a phenomenal task. But it can be done! Computers, sophisticated communications products, and other technologies are being integrated with human resources for creative solutions that lower product costs, improve product and service quality, shorten time to market, improve asset management, and provide insight into unforeseen business opportunities.

This chapter will discuss issues and opportunities that must be considered during the technology assessment process. Some of the more notable publicly discussed applications of integrated technical solutions to competitive business problems are used as examples.

CORPORATE OBJECTIVES

Technology assessment seeks opportunities to match changes in techniques, processes, and equipment to specific business goals and objectives. To accomplish this, however, the technology assessor must have a clear understanding of the client's business. This includes the economic environment, assumptions regarding the firm's customers, the structure of the industry, the product and service offerings that distinguish the firm from its competitors, the processes used to develop and manufacture products, and the cost structure. These business factors can then be related to a set of business drivers, constraints, and opportunities—typically stated in the form of corporate goals and objectives.

The most famous business question remains: What business are we in? From the noted 1960 essay "Marketing Myopia" by Professor Theodore Levitt of Harvard, the answer to this question defines the scope and overall objectives of the enterprise.[1] Professor Levitt originally used the question to show how companies need to define their industries broadly to take advantage of growth opportunities. Referring to the railroad tycoons of the 1930s who, had they been asked the question, would have answered, "The railroad business," Levitt showed how that narrow definition contributed to the inevitable decline of the railroads. Being product-oriented instead of customer-oriented, the railroad tycoons banked on the longevity of their product—trains—and ignored the advances in technology, then represented by airplanes.

Levitt convincingly argued that the tycoons were really in the transportation business, not merely the railroad business. By seeing their market narrowly, the owners and managers of American railroads set their industry on a dead-end track. During the 1940s and 1950s, the mobility of the American public and the need to ship products over greater distances in shorter times, coupled with developments in aeronautics, led to a rapid growth of airlines at the expense of railroads. Had the railroad tycoons seen themselves in the transportation business, that insight might have led them to purchase then-fledgling airlines like Pan Am and TWA.

"Linking two modes of transportation could have made the rail and airline businesses complementary instead of competitive. . . . The railroaders judged the future by the past and largely locked themselves out of the profits to be made from the fantastic mobility of American society," according to Curtis Page and Charles Selden of Pepperdine University.[2]

Questioning the industry and how the firm intends to play a role is now common. Levitt's argument against myopic management is widely quoted, and Harvard has sold well in excess of 265,000 reprints of the original article.[3] Business school graduates are well versed in asking this fundamental question, and managers regularly ask, "What business are we in?" as part of annual goal-setting processes. So finding a written list of the corporate purpose, business philosophies, and overall objectives is typically easy.

We all have seen lists of general business beliefs and objectives bronzed and proudly displayed in the public lobbies of the Fortune 500. From mainstream consumer products leaders to high-tech notables, these operating philosophies and mission statements are visible and become part of their corporate cultures. Well-managed companies foster this understanding among all their employees; indeed, it is one of the reasons for the long-standing success of firms like Procter & Gamble, Johnson & Johnson, Clorox, and Hewlett-Packard. From line technicians to the CEO at Ford, "Quality is Job 1."[4] And regardless of their organizational position or geographic location, managers, technical professionals, and administrative employees of IBM know that "IBM Means Service."[5]

As fundamental as these mission directives are to the firm's view of itself, companies regularly reevaluate them to avoid "marketing myopia." For example, in 1978 the airline industry was deregulated. The regulation-responsiveness of these companies was forced to change to customer-responsiveness. Fare wars, route raiding, acquisitions, and new ways of looking at operations led the airlines to change their focus from transportation to transportation services.[6]

From this basic business framework, the firm's executives develop a dynamic set of strategic plans and tactical goals. This could include some of the following statements:

- Become the low-cost producer.
- Double our growth every ten years.
- Dominate our market segment by obtaining a 37 percent share with 1 percent annual growth.
- Become independent of suppliers within three years by acquiring manufacturing and distribution facilities that will allow price leadership.
- Improve product quality fourfold so we can compete in the luxury goods segment at a premium price.

Companies set and modify objectives and goals regularly. By being in touch with them, technology assessors set the groundwork for understanding the client's business—what drives it and what the firm is trying to accomplish. Each department in the organization develops its own goals and plans ways in which it can contribute to the firm's attainment of its overall objectives. A complete understanding of departmental roles, objectives, and goals is the starting point of an analysis of how technology can be applied toward meeting specific corporate objectives.

ORGANIZATIONAL RECEPTIVENESS

Another subjective assessment that must be made early in the process is the determination of the client's receptivity to exploiting technical change. Obviously no rational business leader implements technology for its own sake; there must be a competitive or operational reason for change. But, on the other hand, knowing the firm's history in successfully (or unsuccessfully) using technology helps frame the range of technical possibilities.

For example, innovative firms are typically willing to invest heavily in new technologies. *Innovators* understand that being the first to adopt technology can help establish new markets, grab market share, establish the rules of competition, and streamline operations. Typically these qualities are found in growing competitive industries, such as high-tech developers and financial services. Their staffs are likely to be computer literate; most communications happen electronically; a few working artificial intelligence projects may be used to augment decisions and control manufacturing; and they are anxious to hear about the latest technical developments. They may also be willing to risk larger projects for potentially greater benefits.

Likewise, *augmentors* are companies that seek a technology modification that enhances their product or service. They may not be interested in discovering new business opportunities and risking larger investments. Technology can be seen in applications that go beyond mechanization of plant and office operations. They may have systems that allow for direct communications with distributors; people use computers for spreadsheets and electronic mail; and a few manufacturing plant robots can be found giving the firm a cost advantage. For the augmentors, smaller projects with calculated risks may be the most reasonable course of action. We describe these firms as those who search for opportunities by drilling many shallow wells rather than one or a few deep ones. Augmentors may be found in mature yet competitive industries such as consumer products, food, and beverages.

The third type of company is the *ultra-conservative*. In such a firm, the extent of technology implementation is likely to be centered on operational aspects of the business, such as financial records and manufacturing processes. Risk aversion and a demand for increased efficiency with a tangible payback typifies conservative companies. They may have a limited history of technology adoption, and the range of solutions the technology assessor can credibly offer is, likewise, limited. Until recently, banks and insurance companies were notoriously conservative. The speed with which financial transactions occur, plus deregulation, has forced these previously conservative companies to become the most innovative of the financial services firms leaving the ultra-conservative label to a dwindling number of organizations, notably public utilities and government services.

Organizational receptiveness to technological change is a key issue that cannot be avoided by the assessment consultant. It will vary along a continuum from the most conservative to the most innovative, from what is typically thought of as "foot-draggers" to "pioneers." Hardly any competent manager has failed to grasp the significance of technology to the bottom line. They have read *In Search of Excellence* and other books from Tom Peters and Robert Waterman, perused *Business Week*, had certain *Computerworld* articles of interest routed to them, and they may make a morning ritual of reading *The Wall Street Journal*.

It is common knowledge among managers that the companies consistently ranked as "excellent" by these industry authorities have at least one thing in common—they demonstrate a willingness to apply innovation and renew themselves. Companies like Hewlett-Packard, Delta Airlines, Johnson & Johnson, and Perdue Farms are leaders in their markets because they foster a tradition of innovation. Procter & Gamble, a company proud of its conservative history, goes the extra mile by forcing innovation and competition among its own brands. One can certainly assume that such internal competition has trickle-down effects to the systems analysts, whereby each analyst seeks technology that will bolster the position of his or her brand against other brands—P&G's or its competitors'.

So it comes as no surprise to managers that industry leaders adopt and exploit technology. Even the most conservative companies are willing to use technology where appropriate. The resistance seems to lie in the corporate culture's acceptance of risk. Technology assessors must determine whether the client firm has a culture that encourages an acceptable level of risk for its expected rewards and whether people can act like entrepreneurs for the betterment of the company. This is a crucial test because the internal systems staff and the technology assessor must be given the opportunity to succeed and to fail. Without the opportunity to fail, there can be no organizational growth—in other words, "no risk, no rewards."

VISIONING

One of the many techniques used during the objectives-setting process is *visioning*. Going beyond goals and tactics to meet today's business objectives, visioning asks the additional question, "What business should the firm be in five years from now?" The answer to this second fundamental business question helps the firm stay flexible enough to adapt to changing customer preferences, economic fluctuations, and new competitors.

Visioning is an exercise that allows managers to anticipate contingencies based on an unconstrained picture of reality. When MIS managers follow the lead of their corporate executives, MIS visioning not only seeks to use technology to support today's goals, but forecasts trends in information technology and develops plans to take advantage of new developments. For example, in the early 1980s, it became clear that American companies needed to trim the fat from overhead and staff organizations to remain cost-competitive. MIS managers envisioned a day, not too far in the future, that the organization would need to be flatter, leaner, and more responsive. Layers of middle managers were expected to disappear. Hierarchical decision making was expected to be replaced with the delegation of responsibility and authority in a matrix organization.

To make this organizational vision a reality, the most progressive MIS managers promoted better desktop decision and communications tools. Since staff analysts would become rare, line managers were introduced to *Lotus 1-2-3* and presentation graphics packages so they could perform their own decision analyses. Easy-to-use database query languages were sought for direct user information access plus (to support an organization where everyone may need to communicate with everyone else) electronic mail and teleconferencing to support a flatter organization.

The MIS vision helps create a cohesive message that focuses programs, technology decisions, resources, and key projects toward a shared view of the future. Visioning ties together the business strategy with the technology architecture (e.g., the systems, network, data sources, and applications). Those aspects of the technology architecture that support the vision are retained; those that detract from it are rejected.

Effective visioning exercises are intensive, lengthy meetings. Usually held offsite, away from normal distractions, technology visioning is a commitment of one to three days to reshape how the firm does business. The key MIS managers, senior technologists, a few of the end users from crucial business functions, and a facilitator typically attend visioning sessions.

The process, in its general form, follows a dialogue in this manner:

1. *Assess the Present Environment.*

     What does our industry look like? Who are the key players?

     What is our business?

     Who are we? What talents do we bring to the table?

     What are we trying to accomplish?

     What gives us our competitive edge?

     What are our current corporate objectives?

     What are the two or three most important business functions in our corporation that are key to meeting these objectives?

     What are MIS's objectives?

     What key projects support the important business objectives?

     What technologies give us a unique product or service advantage?

2. *Forecast the Business Environment of the Future.*

     What does the economy look like? What about demographics?

     What is happening in our industry?

     What fringe developments, if successful, could restructure the industry?

     What will our industry look like five years from now?

     With whom will we compete? What is their advantage?

     What impact will this have on our basic business direction and priorities?

     Why the change?

     How will these changes affect those factors that give us an advantage?

     What must we do to remain special?

     What new opportunities do these changes open up for us?

     How will our company conduct business?

     What is the role of product innovation, efficiency of operations, organizational structure, customer service, and supplier relationships?

     What special skills will we exercise?

     What will be the likely corporate and MIS objectives in the future?

     What key projects will we be working on?

     What capabilities will we need that don't exist today?

3. *Plan Key Technology Investments Required to Support the Vision.*

     Of the key technologies that will be used in the future, assign people to track developments and recommend prototypes.

Identify technologies that could dovetail into a crucial capability that does not exist today; consider pilot or production projects.

Consider restructuring the MIS organization in phases to support efforts that will accomplish the vision.

Develop a technology architecture in broad terms that defines the basic computing, communications network, database standards, and policies that will support the long-term vision.

Plan for the training needed to prepare the staff for accomplishing the vision.

Visioning can be implemented by adopting a forward focus or a backward focus. By looking forward, the firm asks what technologies can help meet the future objectives? A backward focus asks what business objectives can be supported or opportunities opened by taking advantage of our unique technology portfolio? The former seeks to broaden the range of technologies that can positively impact a limited number of business objectives, as seen in Figure 4-1. The latter seeks to broaden the objectives of the enterprise so more of them may be receptive to technology impact, noted in Figure 4-2. A forward focus can lead to a broader portfolio of technologies applicable to the enterprise, while a backward focus can concentrate the firm's resources on a few key technologies that permeate the organization.

It must be remembered that this is an iterative process. Repeat this exercise at least annually and be open to changing it. Of course, visioning should be repeated whenever the objectives or the competitive environment change.

TECHNOLOGY FORECASTING

Because the company's competitive position depends, to at least a moderate degree, on its leadership in one or more applications of technology, foresight about technological matters becomes critical. Even for those companies that are not technological leaders, keeping abreast of trends is an important means of avoiding unpleasant and costly technological surprises. For the analyst or consultant, forecasting the useful life of a particular innovation is yet another important consideration in technology assessment. A useful framework for technology forecasting is the S-Curve.

Advocated by McKinsey & Company's Richard Foster, an S-Curve is a graphical depiction of the relationship between the effort put into improving a product or process and the results the firm gets back for that

Figure 4-1
Forward-Focused Visioning

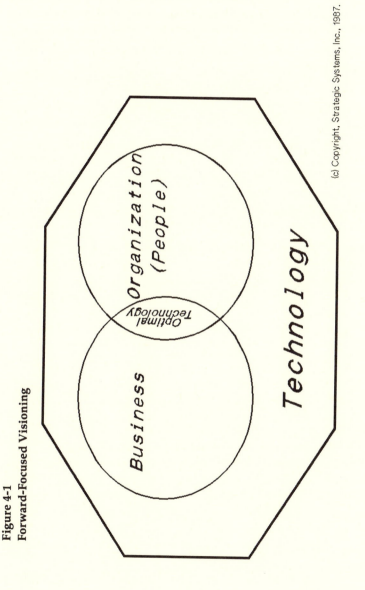

Forward–Focused Visioning asks "What technologies can help meet
future business objectives and organizational needs ?"

Figure 4-2
Backward-Focused Visioning

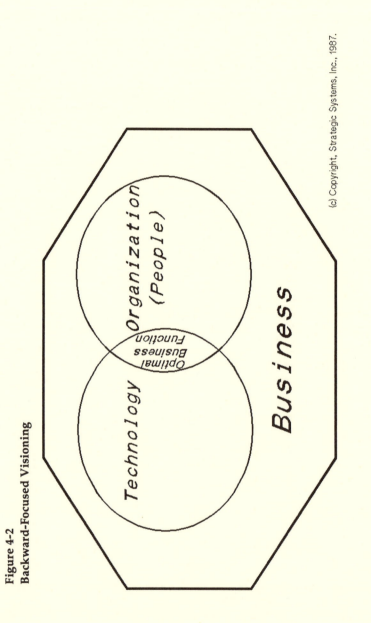

Backward-Focused Visioning asks "What current business objectives

can be leveraged by application of technology ?"

investment.[7] It is called an S-Curve because when the results are plotted, typically an S-shaped graph appears (see Figure 4-3). In non-mathematical terms, the S-Curve shows the life cycle of a particular product or process. In the early stages of development, substantial funds are invested in a new technology, and progress is minimal. As the knowledge and processes used to enhance the technology and successfully apply it develop, there is a period of substantial payback for little additional effort or investment. Finally, as the technology matures, more money and effort will be invested for smaller returns. At this point of maturity, the technology has reached its limit, and new technologies compete with it for dominance and increased performance or returns.

In business, limits determine which technologies, which machines, and which processes are on the verge of obsolescence. Examples from the computer industry abound: TV monitors replaced computer forms in office applications, transistors replaced vacuum tubes, semiconductors outpaced transistors, disk drives replaced magnetic tapes, fiber optics are expected to replace copper wires, and one day optical computers are likely to overshadow electron-based computers. This series of birth, development, maturity, and decline repeats with each technological advance in a seemingly permanent upward spiral of progress.

The key to successful exploitation of technology is managing the inevitable discontinuities. S-Curves typically come in pairs, with one technology outperforming another. When the mature phase of one curve is overshadowed by the innovation phase of a newer, higher performing technology, a discontinuity exists (see Figure 4-4). It is this discontinuity that presents opportunity for exploitation. Companies have been successful at drastically increasing their markets by adopting a new technology at the point of discontinuity. This is what Foster calls the "Attacker." Xerox attacked the carbon-paper makers in the 1960s by developing a more flexible and cheaper duplicating process. IBM outpaced Smith Corona in the office by developing electric typewriters and, subsequently, computer-based word processors. The same could be said for not only the producers of technology but the users as well (as the bank ATM examples show).

The selection of technologies requires knowledge of competing technologies and the talent of foresight. There are no magical rules for success, however. It helps to consider what one is trying to accomplish with a technology—whether the firm seeks efficiency or effectiveness. Efficiency is the slope of the present S-Curve, while effectiveness is related to a determination of which S-Curve the business will pursue (e.g., vacuum tubes vs. solid state).[8] Put another way, we can seek efficient operations by applying an improved version of the same technology, or we can shift to a whole new

Figure 4-3
The S-Curve

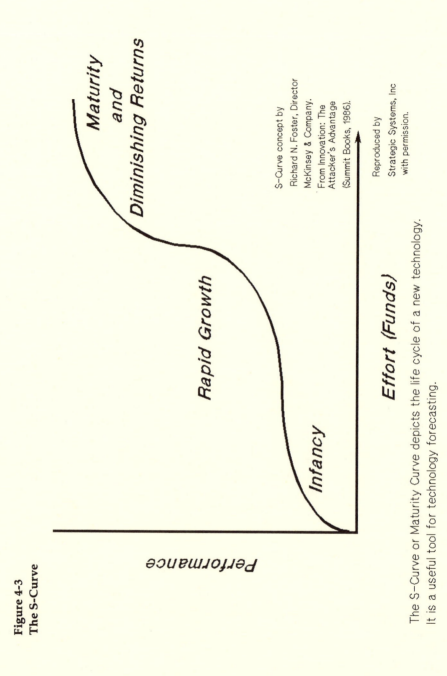

Maturity and Diminishing Returns

Rapid Growth

Infancy

Performance

Effort (Funds)

S–Curve concept by Richard N. Foster, Director McKinsey & Company. From Innovation: The Attacker's Advantage (Summit Books, 1986).

Reproduced by Strategic Systems, Inc with permission.

The S–Curve or Maturity Curve depicts the life cycle of a new technology. It is a useful tool for technology forecasting.

Figure 4-4
Technological Discontinuities

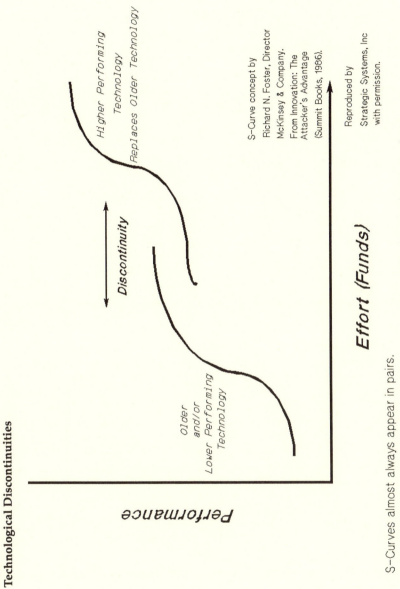

Higher Performing Technology

Replaces Older Technology

Discontinuity

Older and/or Lower Performing Technology

Performance

Effort (Funds)

S-Curve concept by Richard N. Foster, Director McKinsey & Company. From Innovation: The Attacker's Advantage (Summit Books, 1986).

Reproduced by Strategic Systems, Inc with permission.

S-Curves almost always appear in pairs.
Together they represent a discontinuity — when one technology replaces another.

51

magnitude of performance, whereby our effectiveness is changed by a new high performance technology. In this latter case, we are operating on an entirely different S-Curve, and HOW we do business is likely to be very different from our competitors. We have, in effect, gained a competitive advantage through adoption of a new technology and changed the rules of competition in our industry forever.

According to Foster, the key to attacking competitors and defending one's own advantages is in picking the right technology: "Identifying the alternatives and recognizing their limits does not usually lead to an obvious answer. The best strategy may be to pick the adolescent technology with the highest limit because it is never clear when a new technology is really going to emerge."[9]

Foster also gives the following good indications when the current technology may be approaching obsolescence:

1. There is increasing discomfort about the productivity of system developers.
2. Development costs may be increasing, and delays become more common.
3. New applications, innovation, and general creativity wanes.
4. Disharmony and poor morale become evident among the developers.
5. Across-the-board improvements become rare, and system users must be segmented to find productivity increases.
6. There are wide differences in technology spending among competitors that use the same technology, with little or no apparent effects.
7. Frequent changes in management seem to have no impact on technology productivity.
8. Smaller competitors in select niches and/or supposed weaker competitors start succeeding with radical approaches that everyone else says cannot work.[10]

Take the time to ask around the industry or question competing technology vendors on the previous eight areas. When these complaints or troubling observations become apparent, a technology may be reaching its limit. As a technology approaches the top of its S-Curve and gets closer to its performance limits, it takes greater effort or investment to produce even small changes in product or process performance. Selection of a technology in such a state of maturity or decline is tantamount to voluntarily constraining the firm's possibilities and should, generally, be avoided.

S-Curves are useful tools that assist in the selection of the long-term technology portfolio. In the beginning, technologies may be chosen based on influences from the corporate objectives. But in the long run, technology forecasting can also be used as input to the objectives-setting process. S-Curves and the management of discontinuities can point out areas where the firm can take advantage of technical change, thus influencing corporate planning. It is this symbiotic relationship between technology forecasting and corporate planning that demonstrates the true value of S-Curves.

MATCHING TECHNOLOGY
AND PROBLEM STRUCTURE

The skill of managing innovation involves matching the changing requirements of the market and the enterprise with the new possibilities generated by technological advance. One of the challenges, however, is to properly identify what types of problems lend themselves to computer-based solutions. A second problem is derived from the first one. Given that a set of business problems are candidates for some type of automation, how does one decide which type of technology best fits the task at hand?

We have found that competitive problems, management decisions, organizational activities, and business opportunities involve taking some action based on information. In addition, the identified problems, and others, can be characterized along a continuum from highly structured to unstructured. Seen another way, the means to solve these problems range from easy, almost automatic, to difficult and subjective judgments. It is like the difference between a data processing installation deciding whether to add more disk drives and a brand manager deciding whether to sponsor a new TV show. The problems are quite different; information requirements differ by an order of magnitude; and the stakes are higher in the latter case. We have noticed that there is inherently more risk and reward accompanying the important strategic problems of the firm, and these risky problems involve more unstructured decisions. It is therefore important, as part of the technology assessment process, to understand the strengths and limitations of the ways in which technologies can be applied to the entire spectrum of problem categories (see Figure 4-5).

Structured Problems

Computer technology has made its greatest impact on well-structured problems. Historically, these problems may be described in terms of numerical values and have defined goals. They may have, for example, goals of

Figure 4-5
Comparative Business Decisions and Example Technologies

Problem or Decision Type	Business Function	Technology Application
Structured	Accounting Transaction Processing Personnel Records	Batch Data Processing Interactive Query Office Automation
Semi-Structured	Mat'l Req. Planning (MRP) Portfolio Mix "What-If" Questions Distribution Plans	Distributed Processors Distributed Databases Operations Research Decision Support
Unstructured	Plant Location Competitive Strategies Advertising Plans	Heuristic Modeling Artificial Intelligence

Various technologies are better at solving certain types of problems and assisting with certain categories of decisions.

(c) Copyright, Strategic Systems, Inc., 1987.

maximizing profit or minimizing cost, and their parameters (such as raw materials, labor, the cost of capital, and time) have quantitative expressions. Problems with numerical values (such as cubic feet of oil, hours of labor at a defined wage rate, and interest rates) lend themselves to mathematical expression.

Whole academic and professional fields grew as a result of the need to manage these variables—cost accounting and operations research, for instance. Because the rules of decision making for structured problems have been honed down to a predictive science, the associated problem-solving techniques can be easily transmitted to new entrants to the profession. Structured functions, likewise, were some of the first areas of the enterprise to be "automated" with computer-based control systems.

Early data processing applications concentrated, almost exclusively, on automating those functions of the business that were known, predictive, and quantifiable. Industry knew how to take an order, log it in a bookkeeping journal, check inventories, manufacture the product, ship it to the customer, and determine the impact of that shipment on the profit-and-loss position of the company. There was little unknown or subjective about it. What was needed, however, was a means to manage the crushing weight of paperwork and a human bureaucracy that accompanied structured operations as businesses grew into major multinational players. The large data processing systems by IBM, Burroughs, Honeywell, Sperry, and Univac with batch application programs written in COBOL, PL/1, and RPG were highly successful in automating these structured business functions.

Today, these same business problems have become so common that software applications can be purchased on the open market to solve over 90 percent of the cases. Most software packages can be modified for the specific needs of the firm, and, indeed, these modifications and linking these production systems together in unique ways are two of the dwindling ways that a competitive advantage can be obtained from this technology. Batch systems have become a requirement to compete, but since every company has them, it is more difficult to sustain high returns from them. This is a classic case of a mature technology at the top of its S-Curve.

Even though there are decreasing returns to be gained from investments in batch production systems, the firm cannot function without them. They are a given! Such structured problems lend themselves to applications of Management Information Systems (MIS) that not only perform bookkeeping functions but provide exception reports for better control of operations. In addition, batch systems are the fundamental repositories for most of the information on the operations of the firm. In effect, they hold the key to using corporate information for competitive advantage.

So when it comes to assessing a technology for its applicability to a structured problem, consider how the timely use of information from that structure can be used to support semi-structured decisions.

Semi-Structured Problems

Semi-structured problems lie on the continuum between the analytical objectivity of mechanistic structured problems and the intuitive subjectivity of unstructured problems. They are called semi-structured because they may contain certain aspects of both structured and unstructured problems.

They also evolve as by-products of increased knowledge about unstructured problems. It should be remembered that problem experience tends to generate more structure (i.e., problems that once seemed "fuzzy" become more definitive over time). For example, at the turn of the century the process of ordering inventory was relatively unstructured. It was probably handled by a purchasing expert who relied on experience to manage inventories efficiently. When the mathematical formula for the economic order quantity (EOQ) was developed in the 1920s, the art of purchasing inventory became a well-structured technique that has become further refined over the decades with automated technologies.[11]

Therefore, semi-structured problems may involve mechanical decisions like ordering inventory, but they are also likely to have components of the problem that require managerial judgment. These types of problems lend themselves to such technologies as *augmented MIS*. By augmented, we mean that the production systems used for accounting and control of the enterprise are complemented by personal computing resources, decision support tools, spreadsheet modeling packages, advanced graphics, and usable query languages to extract data from databases. (Decision support systems and personal computers will be discussed in more detail in a later section.) Systems for semi-structured problems go beyond reporting data for controlling the enterprise; they augment existing decision processes with new information and allow managers to look at the business from a different angle.

Unstructured Problems

Problems that are not numeric, have no quantitatively defined goals (objective function), and no consistent algorithmic solution can be considered unstructured. Such problems may be ones like those found in the food processing industry—selecting just the right coffee beans for blending or ensuring consistent process control of the ingredients for packaged foods—where the quality of the product depends, to a large extent, on the subjective judgments of experts. Such problems involve decisions where knowledge may be inconsistent (i.e., there may be many ways to solve the problem). Unstructured problems also involve common sense—the ability to know when certain facts are relevant, to act on those facts by framing a solution in symbolic (rather than mathematical) terms, and to know the limits of one's expertise.

Unstructured problems have historically caused difficulty for systems analysts, simply because of their lack of mathematical structure. Computers were seen as numerical processors that could add, subtract, and compare two values. From these basic functions, more sophisticated mathematical manipulations could be performed at nanosecond speeds. But what eluded systems professionals for many years was the ability to capture human expertise and manipulate those learnings symbolically. Today the burgeoning field of *artificial intelligence* (AI), specifically *expert systems*, is gaining a measure of success in addressing these problems and should be considered when performing technology assessment on unstructured problems. (Both AI and expert systems will be addressed in greater detail in later sections.) These technologies lend themselves to unstructured problems, not because they are more readily adaptable, but because the payoff from solving unstructured problems is typically higher, and, as a result, the greater investment of time, money, and expertise can be more easily justified.

Such problems occur at higher levels in the organization, involve greater strategic risk, and have a sense of top management urgency about them. In these cases, AI can help impose structure on problems that seemingly have no structure. Once the imposition of structure occurs, formerly unstructured problems may then be solved using traditional structured methods.

VALUE CHAIN ANALYSIS

One of the most important concepts for identifying opportunities for technology application is the *value chain*. The value chain is a method of linking technology value to the bottom-line results of the business. It goes beyond mere cost-reduction efficiencies (although that is certainly a key element) to identifying those areas of the business where information systems can give the firm an advantage over its competitors in the effectiveness of operations.

The value chain concept has been advocated and widely popularized by noted Harvard Business School professor Michael E. Porter in his landmark text, *Competitive Advantage*.[12] Porter describes how information technology is transforming the nature of products, processes, companies, industries, and the character of competition itself.

The value chain is a tool for analyzing the sources of competitive advantage in a firm and how activities can be integrated. If one looks at the firm as a collection of activities—such as product development, manufacturing, assembly, warehousing, sales force operations, order processing, and post-sale service—one can see how each activity contributes to the firm's competitive advantage (see Figure 4-6). Each activity contributes to the firm's cost position or differentiation. By providing a systematic view of these interdependent business functions, the value chain method uncovers sources of competitive advantage.

Activities in the value chain can be divided into primary and support activities. Primary activities are those involved in physically creating, marketing, and delivering the product. Support activities provide inputs or the infrastructure necessary for primary activities. There are four primary support activities:

1. Procurement of inputs, such as raw materials, subassemblies, and direct machinery used to produce the product,
2. Human resource management in the form of training, development, and compensation effort,
3. Technology development for performing the activity, and
4. The infrastructure of the firm including management overhead.

Activities in the value chain are linked. Each business function is influenced by one or more separate, yet interdependent, functions. For example, the cost of performing one activity is affected by how another is performed. As a result, firms seek to optimize the linkages between activities. But it doesn't stop there. The total enterprise is merely a component in a larger value chain that involves the firm's suppliers, distributors, and ultimately its customers (see Figure 4-7). These linkages must also be coordinated and optimized, and it is one of the reasons companies are developing close business and technological relationships with suppliers and distributors.

Information systems and associated technologies are important because every activity, from designing the product, running the plant, purchasing the inputs, and operating the distribution and service network, requires coordination. Such a high degree of coordination demands information, as Porter and Victor Millar note in a 1985 *Harvard Business Review* article entitled, "How Information Gives You Competitive Advantage."[13] Some of the

Figure 4-6
The Value Chain

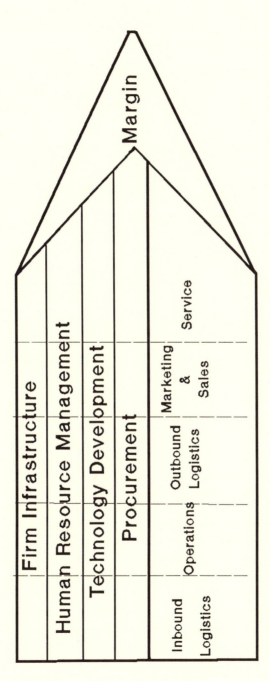

Value Chain concept by Michael E. Porter, (c) copyright 1985.
Adapted from Competitive Advantage by Michael E. Porter,
(The Free Press, A Division of Macmillan, 1985).
Reproduced by Strategic Systems with permission.

Figure 4-7
The Value System (Single Industry Firm)

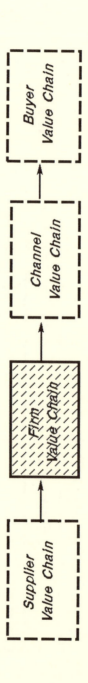

Value Chain concept by Michael E. Porter, (c) copyright 1985.
Adapted from Competitive Advantage by Michael E. Porter,
(The Free Press, A Division of Macmillan, 1985).
Reproduced by Strategic Systems with permission.

technologies that help provide and manage that information are shown in Figure 4-8.

Not only is information needed for coordination, each activity creates and uses information. For example, a distribution function needs information from the finished goods inventory database, and it produces a shipment record that is used by other value activities, such as the accounts receivables and customer service functions. Therefore, information technology fundamentally affects every activity of the firm. It creates powerful impacts on the way activities are structured and the way business functions are linked together.

To use value chain analysis effectively in identifying strategic technology application areas, Porter suggests that internal and external activities be examined for their value contributions to customers. This is crucial because the firm's impact on the value chains of its buyers ultimately determines the success of the enterprise.

The value of the product to customers can be enhanced by embedding advanced technologies in products, and new services can be offered, further differentiating the firm's offerings from its competitors'. Cars with computer interface units that allow for better diagnosis and maintenance, computers that perform their own fault checking, and "smart cards" used by consumers to improve access to funds and leveraging of those funds are examples of increased value and differentiation via technology.

To the manufacturer, technology also becomes important to the extent that it can lower the cost or raise the performance of the firm's products and services relative to its competition. Information technology can be applied to the firm's value chain activities to also give an advantage to the early adopter. Such was the case for banks that adopted ATMs before their competitors and thus gained a permanent market share lead. New technologies can improve the industry structure, enhancing the positions of all companies in the industry. Grocery store checkout scanners, direct linkages to customer bank accounts for debits, and electronic data interchange between chain stores and suppliers are examples of this. So are automated flight reservation systems used by airlines. They are commonplace, but their effect has been to increase the competitiveness and customer service level of the industry.

New flexible manufacturing techniques can reduce the economies-of-scale advantages of dominant competitors, thereby opening the industry to smaller, potentially more creative, entrants. Entry barriers can also be raised by technology. For example, in some distribution industries the automation of materials handling has raised the cost of doing business. What were once general purpose warehouses have now become capital-intensive, special-

Figure 4-8
Representative Technologies in a Firm's Value Chain

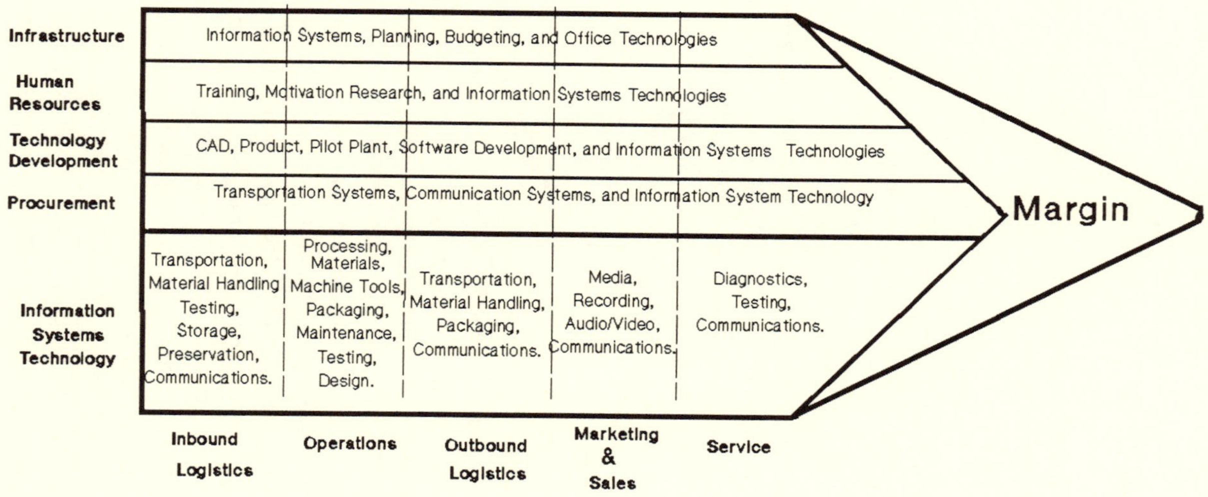

Infrastructure	Information Systems, Planning, Budgeting, and Office Technologies			
Human Resources	Training, Motivation Research, and Information Systems Technologies			
Technology Development	CAD, Product, Pilot Plant, Software Development, and Information Systems Technologies			
Procurement	Transportation Systems, Communication Systems, and Information System Technology			
Information Systems Technology				
Transportation, Material Handling, Testing, Storage, Preservation, Communications.	Processing, Materials, Machine Tools, Packaging, Maintenance, Testing, Design.	Transportation, Material Handling, Packaging, Communications.	Media, Recording, Audio/Video, Communications.	Diagnostics, Testing, Communications.
Inbound Logistics	**Operations**	**Outbound Logistics**	**Marketing & Sales**	**Service**

Value Chain concept by Michael E. Porter, (c) copyright 1985.
Adapted from Competitive Advantage by Michael E. Porter,
(The Free Press, A Division of Macmillan, 1985).
Reproduced by Strategic Systems with permission.

ized facilities.[14] These and other impacts of computer-based technologies that will be described in this chapter are, in essence, what I mean by competitive advantage.

Operational Efficiency

The value chain method of technology assessment seeks to lower the costs or raise the performance of the firm's offerings or both. It is the cost-reduction issue to which I now turn. The most common applications of computers and associated technologies have been where highly structured tasks are found in an organization—for example, the factory floor. The data processing industry was justified more than thirty years ago by the potential of computer automation to reduce costs and improve efficiency in highly structured settings. The natural extension of computer-based automation beyond the factory is the office. From mechanization of routine accounting tasks to improving the efficiency of document preparation, these structured office tasks join factory automation as being among the easily identifiable areas affecting the bottom line of a business that is competing on a cost basis.

Factory Automation

A report by the consulting and market research firm International Data Corporation (IDC) paints a bleak picture for American industry. "[The] American industrial enterprise stands besieged. Foreign competition challenges the dominance of U.S. industrialists, the world no longer plays by America's rules. . . . At issue: bare, basic survival."[15]

The report goes on to cite how American manufacturers suffer from raw material price hikes, labor costs that doubled between 1960 and 1981, and how offshore rivals have mastered the ability to boost product quality and radically cut inventory levels. Victims of this pummeling include the auto, electronics, textile, and machine tool industries.

We are in a position of having to trim flabby organizations, reinvest in new manufacturing plants, and work smarter. Factory automation has been rekindled as a means for the survival of U.S. manufacturing. Of course, automation has been around American industry for a long time, but the key difference now is our collection of new computer and communications-based tools. Collectively, they may be called CIM (*computer integrated manufacturing*).

CIM facilitates sprinting to market with new products and services, reducing manufacturing costs by reducing defects and improving quality, and providing a means for the organization to quickly adapt its processes to new products and changing volumes. The theme underlying CIM is integration. Manufacturing is viewed as a single flow process, highly tuned with no slack time, a rededication to quality, and working smarter with the aid of computers and databases that are shared and updated in real time. CIM goes beyond the factory floor to integrate information in the engineering design office, sales offices, and corporate headquarters. CIM becomes the central nervous system of the enterprise. It is adaptable, decentralized, and built on the information infrastructure provided by computer networking.

Networking and powerful distributed computer workstations tuned for engineering applications allow designers to speed products to market and improve quality by designing quality into the product up front. For example, Hughes Aircraft uses a computer-aided design software product that analyzes thermal conditions in circuits while they are under design. The system highlights areas where cooling may be inadequate. Failure rates of major electronic components such as resistors, capacitors, and semiconductors increase with the temperature. The impact of this physical phenomenon is shown by a 1985 Department of Defense study, which found that failure rates in semiconductors as much as halved for each 10-degree Celsius drop in temperature. It also found that temperature caused more electronic failures than any other single environmental condition—including vibration and humidity. One program involving 200 military aircraft resulted in an estimate of $10 million in maintenance and repair savings for each 5-degree Celsius drop in coolant temperature.[16] With such savings at stake for a seemingly simple solution, it comes as no surprise that engineers at Hughes are encouraged to consider thermal reduction steps during the design phase instead of having to fix failures later.

Error-free designs save money because they do not have to be revised further down the line. When a company simulates manufacturing operations on a computer and simulates product performance stress points, quality can be built in, thus eliminating the need for expensive manufacturing, rework, and redesign. Computer-aided design (CAD) also reduces the number of prototypes a developer must build. For example, 3M sliced six months off the three years it usually takes to develop a microfilm reader because the model designed on a computer was good enough to proceed directly into production.[17]

CAD allows large engineering teams to share common data, ensuring that standard parts are used. *CAE* magazine reports that for a typical engineering company only 20 percent of the parts required for a product are new designs. Forty percent are modifications to existing parts, and another 40 percent are identical to existing parts.[18] A common database of standard parts and its associated instantaneous update of modified parts allows engineers to work with the latest version of information and reduces the chance of mismatched parts. The ability to find existing standard parts also saves design time and paperwork. A common database, when modified, creates a ripple effect of standards throughout the organization. In addition, by tying the engineering database into the network, large companies that source thousands of parts from external suppliers benefit from direct communications of design changes to the companies that manufacture those products. CAD and networking streamline the entire design and procurement process while reducing overall time to market for new products.

Access to engineering databases by manufacturing departments is another facet of CIM. Manufacturing personnel can provide feedback to engineers early in the design process and reduce the risk of specifying products that can't be made. From a high-quality design, the manufacturing department can transfer specifications to factory control computers. These systems oversee standard machines such as welders, sprayers, extruders, assemblers, and generic industrial robots that can be programmed to perform a wide range of operations. In effect, the whole CIM process stresses flexible manufacturing based on shared engineering and sales order data.

In contrast to the traditional hierarchical manufacturing plant that seeks to maximize the use of expensive single-purpose machinery with products going through various stages and specialized plant departments, flexible manufacturing uses programmable machines in work groups called "cells" to produce a wider range of products with reduced set-up times. CIM calls for a shift from manufacturing large lots to small batch production. This often means reducing the amount of time it takes to set up equipment and reconfigure the production plant. It means shifting from a plant that focuses on equipment arranged by function to one in which each production line or cell produces a different part or group of parts in sequence.

Instead of planning for the extensive cost of on-site inventory to feed manufacturing processes, the CIM concept employs *JIT* (*Just-In-Time*) production techniques. This simple technique calls for having materials ready at each point in the manufacturing process, just in time to be used. This is especially important in the electronics industry, where the Institute of Electrical and Electronic Engineers (IEEE) reports that up to 90 percent of the cost of making electronic products is attributed to materials.[19] JIT challenges firms to produce and deliver finished goods just in time to be sold; subassemblies just in time to be assembled into finished goods; fabricated parts just in time to go into subassemblies; and purchased materials just in time to be fabricated.[20]

JIT challenges management to eliminate the slack time in manufacturing. As a result, inventory costs are reduced, and high-volume plants can occupy smaller physical spaces. To pull it off, companies are investing in integrated computer databases and communications networking products to complement materials requirements planning (MRP) software systems.

The CIM approach to quality can be summed up by the phrase, "Do it right the first time." Instead of tolerating the massive costs of scrap and rework, the CIM concept has proven that correcting the manufacturing process at its source is far less expensive in the long run than merely allowing for a certain percentage of defective products. Quality becomes the total philosophy and life blood of the organization. It starts when the manufacturer chooses a small group of key suppliers who abide by strict quality standards such that no defects are delivered to the plant. This eliminates incoming inspection of goods from suppliers. CIM also advocates full shutdown of the production line by the line operators, if necessary, to expose and fix quality problems. Quality production is enhanced by extensive inspection of each component (not merely a sample) with sophisticated technologies.

The inspection technologies range from simple speech recognition systems that keep human inspectors' eyes and hands free, to infrared analyzers that spot thermal stresses in fabricated metals, to expert systems with monitors embedded in devices that help diagnose equipment problems. Another example of quality testing at the source is Hewlett-Packard's showcase artificial intelligence application. An internal system that recognizes patterns in electronic circuit boards and compares them with the stored knowledge of several photolithography engineers, HP's *Photolithography Advisor*, helps reduce wafer quality problems, is always available, and can operate in sterile environments.[21]

Using CIM and JIT techniques, Hewlett-Packard's Cupertino, California, plant was able to reduce the time it takes to assemble a set of thirty-one circuit boards from fifteen days in 1982 to just over eleven hours in 1986. Inventories of the boards were reduced from $670,000 to $20,000, and the number of back orders was reduced from an average of 200 to 2.[22] Digital Equipment Corporation reduced the work-in-process inventory of Winchester disk drives from $5 million to $900,000 at its Colorado Springs facility; IBM's Oswego, New York, plant experienced a 60 percent reduction in inventory; and Motorola's Seguin, Texas, electronic controller plant reported a 75 percent reduction, according to a report by Nhora Cortes-Comerer for the IEEE.[23]

With a creative combination of inspection and monitoring technologies, zero defects from suppliers, JIT production for inventory reduction, flexible manufacturing that quickly responds to engineering changes, and a quality driven organization, American industry can recapture its competitive spirit. However, without the integration of various computer, communications, and electronic sensor technologies, CIM would remain an unfulfilled dream of visionaries.

Office Productivity

Operational efficiencies and associated cost reductions are not limited to the factory. Technology assessors are finding creative ways to affect the overhead of the enterprise by examining the office environment. Here are a few examples.

"Telephone tag" is being dealt a severe blow. *Electronic mail (E-Mail)* provides an almost instantaneous postal service for internal documents, report distribution, new product announcements, and short messages. *Voice mail*, likewise, is enhancing the usefulness of the telephone—what Arthur Andersen's David Rappaport calls the "professional appendage."[24] Since studies show that up to 75 percent of all business calls are not completed on the first try and that the majority of intracompany telephone calls do not require an immediate response, these tools hold the promise of vastly improving personal productivity at a reasonable cost and with simple technology.

The store-and-forward nature of such systems means that, for example, one can write and send a message from a portable computer in a New York airport phone booth at midnight, and the host E-Mail computer in Chicago will receive the message instantly and hold it until the recipient in San Francisco signs on to the system in the morning and retrieves the message. The traveling professional can send the same message to a manager thousands of miles away in San Diego. Because she works late at night and happens to be using the system from a personal computer (PC) at home, the E-Mail system will signal her that new mail has arrived. It will note that it is only a copy of a memo sent to the development manager and that it probably is not urgent. Because it isn't urgent, she can file it in an electronic "to read" file for tomorrow.

She has just completed a ten-page report on her PC and is anxious to call it a night. But before turning in, she sends a copy of the report via electronic mail to her secretary. The secretary will receive the document in the morning and will print a final letter-quality copy for distribution. Because the company's physical mail usually takes a day or so to deliver hardcopy reports, she also sends the traveler an electronic draft copy for review. The traveler can print it off tomorrow in a London hotel room before the big meeting and be well prepared.

Such a scenario is common for electronic mail users. Many organizations are finding that the productivity gain of allowing people to get messages quicker, share ideas freely, reduce the need to travel as often, and get faster turnaround on draft proposals makes E-Mail, such as the *Wang OFFICE* product, a standard offering. Distributed organizations such as Hewlett-Packard have found it a necessary tool to tie together its 60,000 users in thirty-one countries. The internal HP network processes over 9 million screens worth of data per month.[25] In a company with autonomous divisions, the tendency to duplicate effort is decreased by keeping project and product managers in daily contact via E-Mail. Draft documents can be edited by a team of people dispersed over a site or over continents.

HP provides its internal electronic mail software to customers as a product called *HP Desk* with *HP Mail*. Together HP's office products allow messages to be routed throughout a distributed network of minicomputers to recipients based on names and distribution lists. Recipient locations are determined by *HP Mail*, and the system helps determine the correct recipient by displaying for the sender a list of similar names when there may be ambiguities.

Digital Equipment Corporation, another company famous for its distributed structure, offers an electronic desk product called *ALL-IN-1*. Word processing, spelling checker, and a basic function calculator are added to an electronic mail product that communicates with remote DEC *VAXs* and IBM mainframe electronic mail users via a gateway.

ALL-IN-1 has an interactive calendar that allows users to check the availability of other members of the work group, set tentative meeting times, and automatically ask other participants to verify the meeting time. It also features *videotext* and electronic conferencing. Videotext provides E-Mail users the ability to link into external news databases for an online update of current events, stock prices, and internal news such as product announcements, personnel policy listings, and price updates.

Major business opportunities are being realized by established news organizations such as Dow-Jones and Gannett, and by information brokers such as Mead Data Central. Just as *ALL-IN-1*'s videotext taps into outside news sources, Dow Jones electronically distributes *The Wall Street Journal*, Gannett the *USA Today Update*, and Mead provides an electronic database to attorneys called *LEXIS*. These videotext services may be accessed from a home personal computer or an office workstation.

Electronic conferencing is an ongoing dialogue among a group of users on a single topic. Membership is managed by a conference leader, and an electronic meeting is carried on over time. This is an excellent way for new research ideas to be tossed around among a limited group of people.

A technology related to videotex is *text retrieval*—an area of special interest and expertise of Strategic Systems and, specifically, for me. Text retrieval seeks to blend the learnings of the computer industry with the art of the librarian. Still in its infancy, text retrieval has only begun to tap its potential applications. Basically, reports are stored in large electronic databases and are made accessible via PCs or terminals. Typically indexed based on the knowledge of a professional indexer or librarian and once in digitized form, thousands of reports can be scanned for key words and key concepts. The researcher starting a new project can compile a hardcopy collection of all pertinent information on the subject. This reduces duplicate efforts by "reinventing the wheel" and is a favorite of scientists.

Today, business managers are using text retrieval services like *NEXIS* to obtain Wall Street analysts' reports on all companies doing business in a hot new area, to track the product announcements of competitors, and to build dossiers of all articles written about key executives before meeting them.

Systems researchers are applying artificial intelligence techniques to do a better job of getting the right articles for the right people based on interest and project relevancy. They are also using natural language techniques to reduce the volume of irrelevant information. An example of one such system is *CoalSORT*. A knowledge-based interface added to a text database retrieval system, *CoalSORT* facilitates the use of bibliographic databases specific to coal technology. Developed at Carnegie Mellon University by Ira Monarch and Jaime Carbonell, *CoalSORT* uses a knowledge base built by consulting with catalyst and coal experts. The expert knowledge is used to increase the probability that a document cited will be relevant to the user's project interests. The interactive system also gives the user a chance to peek at the document indexing information so a final scan can be made by the human user.[26]

Still a bit crude, *CoalSORT* is the parent of future systems that could assist in the design of coal liquefaction processes. The system allows users to examine full text reports instead of just bibliographies. Such systems could point researchers in the right direction, reduce effort on previously unsuccessful prototypes, shorten the start-up time of new projects, and decrease the training time of new staff members. It also reduces time wasted at the beginning of new projects by staffers who routinely plow through documents searching for relevant articles. No longer will researchers have to read all the articles to decide if they are relevant.

Personal computers are the tools of individual productivity and increased effectiveness. PCs give each user access to corporate data, such as shipping records for a product, customer purchases, and inventory, and facilitate the sharing of expensive peripherals, such as large laser printers, plotters, and optical disks. Data can be analyzed based on personal thinking styles, and "what-if" questions may be asked. Software exists to automate budgets, forecast orders, and spot trends and opportunities in untapped markets. Expert systems can even help in sizing up an opponent before entering negotiations. Word processing decreases the turnaround time for proposals and encourages multiple authorship of reports. Of the $42 billion spent on hardware by U.S. businesses in 1986, more than half went to pay for microcomputers and other small system products.[27] So PCs are likely to be the personal workstations and electronic desks for managers and professionals for some time to come.

The use of friendlier computer-to-user interfaces may be seen by the use of *Windows*, by Microsoft, and *icons*, pioneered by Xerox and Apple Computer. These easy-to-use graphical interfaces eliminate the need for computer users to learn complicated command interfaces. With icons, the user points at a representative picture of the task to be performed, and windowing allows the user to use the computer like a desktop. Just as more than one piece of paper is on a manager's desk at a time, windows allows the computer to work on more than one task at a time. Like icons, windowing uses a simple graphical screen for commands via a pointing device called a *mouse*.

Desktop publishing is a growing area where managers and professionals have realized that the visual esthetics of a report have a good deal to do with its credibility and the reader's retention of the subject matter. Combining a sophisticated word processor with graphics, pictures, numerical manipulation, and a mini-typesetting page composition software product, desktop publishing is a single user activity being performed on PCs and technical workstations.

According to a survey by Interconsult, a Cambridge, Massachusetts, research firm, 60 percent of the Fortune 1000 said they would enter into electronic publishing; 47 percent were planning to buy whole minicomputer-based (not PC) systems; and 31 percent were planning to purchase PC-based pagination software.[28] Companies such as Interleaf, whose product runs on engineering workstations, and Aldus, whose *PageMaker* product is the leader in the PC market, provide individual users the ability to produce professional quality reports, newsletters, and presentations.

There are even inexpensive devices that attach to the PC and produce high-quality 35mm slides for presentations. The traditional methods include sending artwork out to service bureaus and graphic artists or taking a photograph of a PC's screen. The latter method produces poor quality slides, and the former can be quite expensive. The *ImageMaker* by Presentation Technology, Inc., is an IBM-PC based slide maker that uses typesetting and plotter technology to reproduce the screen image with higher resolution than conventional photos.[29]

Empirical research by Jonathan Morell, a social psychologist at the Oak Ridge National Laboratory, and James Leemon, director of organizational research at Consultation Systems, Inc., shows that desktop publishing has the potential to awaken dormant productivity opportunities. Morell and Leemon studied the impact of workstations capable of integrating text, graphics, project management, analysis, and communications functions on a large engineering design firm.

Their results indicate that document quality improved; greater detail was included in documents; in addition, graphs and charts had better content (more meaning). Seventy percent of the users noted that they now do jobs they could not do without the workstation. Eighty-five percent are doing work faster; 64 percent have received new work assignments; and 32 percent have taken the additional step of developing new applications at the workplace. The research also indicates that the workstations may have sparked a spontaneous consolidation of tasks. Work previously done by many people is now being done by fewer people, not because of any conscious reorganization, but because of a natural interaction between the nature of people's jobs and the capacity of the new technology.[30]

Desktop publishing is entering an era of multiple print media, leaving paper as merely one of many options. Since many of today's networks cannot ship compound documents with graphic images produced by desktop publishing, the growth of facsimile machines will continue. Japanese and European companies have used fax machines for years and now American firms have finally embraced this simple technology in a big way.[31] Looking like a desktop copier with a built-in telephone, the fax can speed compound documents around the world in the most timely and cost-effective manner. Attorneys use them to send legal documents; architects send plans; and advertising agencies send brochures and ad copy to clients for review.

In an interview with the *San Francisco Chronicle*, a vice president and counsel for Union Bank noted how he uses his fax to review legal documents and correspondence two or three times a day. Prior to fax, the counsel used to advise the bank's loan officers over the phone about proposed letters to clients who may have fallen behind in their loan payments. He had to visualize what the document looked like and either make a decision or force a delay. Now with fax, he cites cases where a potential delay of two to three days to review actual letters has decreased to the time it takes to fax a document and read it.[32]

A typical document sent coast to coast costs about 50 cents a page for telephone charges and 5 cents for the paper. That certainly beats the prices of the costly overnight delivery services. More than the cost savings, use of the

FAX reduces the turnaround time for delivering important documents and for banking and legal applications. They also show signatures adding to the validity of data and confidence of customers and clients.

Handwritten information has been a long-standing problem for computers. However, advances in *optical character recognition (OCR)* technology is making inroads. Consider the Federal Aviation Administration's (FAA) substantial payroll input. Every other week, 28,000 handwritten time and attendance forms are submitted to the FAA's Atlanta office. Keypunching, validating, and editing would overwhelm the staff. With a *CompuScan Laser Data Entry System* and a Perkin Elmer superminicomputer, the FAA now uses scanners to read hand-printed information from standard forms at about 375 forms per hour. Manual entry at this rate would require six to nine technicians. The OCR device has an error rate of 2 to 5 percent and signals an operator when it cannot recognize a character. The operators are freed to work on more interesting jobs; there is less fatigue and sick time; and payroll technicians now handle 900 accounts each compared with 600 accounts before the OCR.[33]

Strategic Effectiveness

Computers are common tools for improving the productivity and efficiency of highly structured factory and office operations. They are now reaching beyond these traditional arenas to impact non-structured aspects of doing business. Areas such as improving customer satisfaction, increasing market share with better information, providing insight to marketing managers on better ways to target and retain customers, and providing leverage in supplier relationships are among the most promising opportunities to increase effectiveness and generate higher revenue streams.

Communications Enhance Operations and Product Introductions

No discussion of computers applied to value chain activities could rationally proceed without addressing what has become the rallying cry of the industry—networking. The ability of computers to communicate instructions, share files, invoke application programs dispersed over the network, and tie the corporate information resources together rests squarely with its information infrastructure provided by computer networking. We can no more expect information gains without an adequate infrastructure than we could expect an expanded economy during the Industrial Revolution without vast networks of transportation rails, highways, and sea lanes.

The lack of multivendor networking capabilities was cited by *Business Week* as one of the primary causes for the severe computer industry slow-down in 1985-1986. Companies spent the seventies buying hardware, only to find that they were building autonomous applications, referred to as "Islands of Automation." As a result, corporate executives decided to take a long hard look at the value of the promised information resource. This is why major computer vendors embarked on a "bet-the-company" attempt to develop comprehensive data communications products that tie together, first of all, their own equipment and, second, other vendors' products.

Multivendor networking is demanded by large companies and the government because investments in those autonomous information islands must be protected. Standards committees were formed to make connecting two vendors' computers as easy as plugging in jacks in a stereo system. (Ah, if it were only that simple!) Single vendor proprietary systems are definitely out. Even the power of IBM with host systems in well over 80 percent of the Fortune 500 cannot, nor should they, change the current drive toward multivendor integration.

In fact, some companies are finding that a historically hierarchical organization like IBM may not be the best company to implement computer networking for a distributed processor, diverse application, multivendor environment. MIS managers understand that IBM and other mainframe vendors, such as Amdahl and NEC, make most of their hardware profits from mainframe sales and that distributed processing could come slowly to firms that see the decentralization of information as a bite at the hand that feeds it.

In addition, IBM's difficulty at integrating its own processor families was an indication to MIS managers that multivendor networking might never happen if left solely to the computer giant. This has not gone unnoticed by IBM's competitors. Digital, Hewlett-Packard, Wang, Data General, and AT&T, plus makers of smaller systems such as Apple, Apollo, and SUN Microsystems, have all made a valiant stab at some form of *distributed data processing (DDP)*. A hearty cadre of specialized networking vendors, such as Ungermann-Bass and INI, grew to prominence by bridging the communications gaps caused by the major computer companies.

The networking behind DDP must, by definition, support decentralized decision making. Power must be given to end users and to remote functional units of the organization. Although IBM is making strides in this decentralized direction with its announcement of new mid-range processors and network protocols such as *LU6.2* and *SAA (Systems Applications Architecture)*, which allows peer-to-peer networking of its processors and applications, it still has a very long way to go before we see a pervasion of true DDP throughout its product families.

What leading-edge companies want is (borrowing a phrase from the World Future Society) to be able to think globally, but act locally. They want to control the information base as a corporate asset but also have the autonomy to make decisions locally without begging on bent knee to corporate MIS departments. Competitive pressures force companies to keep a corporate perspective. They must maintain an effective and frequently accessed communications channel with key corporate resources in marketing and various technical expertise areas. Communications is needed horizontally with other divisions. They need to take advantage of local suppliers, tailor offerings to local customers, and actively manage those business factors that directly affect them. Most important, they must be able to quickly adapt to a changing business environment. With this as a backdrop, even though Fortune 500 companies are not about to leave the fold of IBM, they are seeking vendors known for their decentralized approach to computer networking. Companies with the edge are paraphrasing the World Future Society's slogan to read: Keep on a corporate hat, but by all means take local action.

Distributed processing by means of advanced computer networking can benefit a wide range of organizations. Linking offices to remote shipping, receiving, warehousing, and manufacturing facilities is common. Growing in popularity is networking among producers, suppliers, and distributors; among design engineers and factory floors; and among hospital administrators, physicians, and patients.

Tying distributed computers together and facilitating such advanced communications are *local area networks (LANs)* and their remote cousins, *wide area networks (WANs)*. A typical LAN is Ethernet. Developed in the 1970s by Xerox, Intel, and Digital Equipment Corporation, Ethernet provides common physical cables and hardware interfaces for interconnection of computer products from multiple vendors. Coupled with vendor-supplied software, Ethernet services allow files to be transferred between systems, programs on one system to invoke processes on another system, and terminal users to access data on any system on the LAN (not just the one to which the terminal is attached). This peer-to-peer access to programs, processes, data, peripherals, and specialized computers allows organizations to tailor smaller machines to specific applications.

Rather than settling for the mediocrity of all users sharing a common large computing monolith and competing for resources, distributed processors on LANs allow the engineering department to select the right system for its purposes while the finance department optimizes its system for accounting and analysis. Although each department chooses its own computing resources, LANs tie the total organization together to form the image of a system larger than the corporate mainframe. Total processing power for the collective LAN exceeds that of a mainframe. Sharing of expensive peripherals such as laser printers and optical disks is enhanced, and access to high-speed "compute servers" for sophisticated mathematical analysis is allowed from remote locations. In effect, the network becomes the system (paraphrasing Digital's popular slogan).

With LANs, a typical commercial business with shipping, receiving, inventory, and a shop floor can monitor work flows from the receipt of raw materials, through manufacturing and inventory to receipt of payment. Modems attached to terminal servers on the LAN permit remote offices or sales representatives to use portable terminals or personal computers to call in orders or check on accounts in seconds. Engineering departments can get feedback on designs directly from marketing databases. Modified designs can be transferred to manufacturing and incorporated in flexible manufacturing operations. Buildings may be wired with LANs to take advantage of energy and environmental management systems. University campuses are supported by LANs providing remote access to library reference works and transmitting video-based instructional programs. Hospitals may connect laboratory testing facilities to doctors' offices, and nurses may monitor patients' vital signs and view the most critical patients from a single console using teleconferencing.

WANs are sophisticated public and private communications networks that provide the features and services of LANs over a widely dispersed area. From campuses to cities to continents, WANs use microwaves, fiber optics, high-grade long distance telephone lines, and satellites to provide virtually unlimited access to organizational information resources.

Satellites are very costly and are typically justified by the largest of organizations who have massive amounts of data to transmit over vast distances. Cost-effective alternatives are appearing, however. AT&T, American Satellite Corporation and Houston International Teleport, to name a few, are jockeying for market position in a potentially lucrative segment—public satellite services—which amounted to a $1 billion market in 1987 alone.[34] For many companies with expensive leased lines or for those who need to transfer not only data, but voice and video, sharing time on a public satellite may be quite attractive.

The cost of communications is being easily justified by the benefits of more effective human interactions. Research by Tom Allen, a professor at MIT's Sloan School of Management, suggests that new information system technologies (such as electronic mail, electronic conferencing, and distributed project management tools) can substitute for organizational structures, thereby allowing greater flexibility in choosing personnel and technical specialties for projects. Allen explains that most scientific and engineering departments are organized along the lines of either (1) technical discipline or (2) project teams that produce deliverable products. Some firms find that the effectiveness of technical professionals is enhanced by keeping people of like disciplines located near each other to share ideas and stay abreast of the latest developments in their areas of expertise. He calls this type of organization "input-focused." Its alternative, the "output-focused" organization, is the traditional project team—a diverse mix of people with various specialties managed by a team leader with definite project objectives and a structured time frame for deliverables.[35]

The input-focused organization enables effective communication within a discipline but causes a barrier to the coordination of projects. Output-focused organizations get the task done but run the risk of isolating specialists who need a close-knit group of colleagues to add value to the project by bringing to the table unique knowledge and skills. The firm is left with an unpleasant trade-off. The structure needed in many of today's dynamic organizations requires a blend of technical expertise and efficient management of people toward a goal.

Electronic communication allows companies to organize in either way and minimizes the effect of such a forced trade-off. Members of the project team (output-focused) may use electronic mail to stay in touch with colleagues, electronic conferencing to pull together geographically dispersed groups of specialists around a common topic, and database retrieval systems to browse libraries and obtain copies of pertinent research reports. Departments organized by discipline can now use electronic mail to stay in contact with a physically disjointed project team. Status reports on specific subtasks may be shared, and the project manager may use PERT and GANT chart applications on a shared electronic mail system to keep track of the subtasks and send requests and feedback on progress (or lack thereof) to individual members of a team. It is no longer necessary to enforce strict geographical or organizational rules on the productivity or the creative expertise of project members.

Does communicating more effectively really pay off? According to Frank Giannantonio, director of information services for Avon, it definitely does. "There's been a 23 percent productivity gain among managers and for secretarial and administrative staff a 53 percent increase," Giannantonio states in a recent ad for Digital Equipment Corporation's networking products.[36]

In another case, Washington Mutual Savings Bank of Seattle installed mainframe links to its microcomputers that are used by loan processors.

Since loans are processed by several people working on different sections that may originate at a branch office, the bank needed to insure an easy information flow among all the loan processors. A common database of loan applications can be accessed by each of the loan processors. This balanced the workload and insured the accuracy during a record year in mortgage volume. The processing and closing time was decreased, and the lending office was able to increase the mortgages granted.[37]

The distributed networking philosophy of thinking globally but acting locally demonstrates concrete benefits, even beyond those mentioned earlier in this section. By giving users control over their data and their applications, rather than centralizing computing with the MIS function that may not know their business, Johnson & Johnson was able to facilitate R&D scientists' insight into physical processes from tests that are hard to repeat. The documentation of the array of tests required by the Food and Drug Administration to introduce a new pharmaceutical product is staggering. The compliance cycle usually takes five to seven years. With advanced computer-based applications owned and run by the R&D staff, J&J was able to cut a year or more off that cycle.[38]

In a business where a new drug may bring in $50 million to $100 million in sales in its first year, time to market is crucial. Every day a pharmaceutical company delays an introduction can cost $1 million to $2 million in lost revenue and a lower market share. Networking provides the "data highway" or the infrastructure that allows distributed computer-based applications to garner such benefits for progressive organizations.

Suppliers, Distributors, and Customers

Technology assessors can use value chain analysis to seek ways in which new information management technologies can change relationships between buyers and sellers. The most obvious impact of this kind of technology leverage has been a reduction in the number of intermediaries—for example, wholesalers, distributors, agents, and so-called middle men. Transactions that took several steps before are now taking two and will take one step tomorrow. This permits buyers and sellers to conduct transactions directly, quickly, and at a lower cost.

Service industries are the immediate beneficiaries (or losers, depending on your perspective). Stocks can be bought and sold electronically without registered brokers; airline ticket purchases no longer need travel agents; international calls can be made without telephone operators; and banking is routinely done without the assistance of human tellers. These examples of consumer services will be common to most readers. Less obvious but of more strategic importance to corporations is the impact technology has on shifting the basis of supplier power.

According to Michael Porter, "A firm's procurement and inbound logistics activities interact with a supplier's order entry system . . . [to] provide opportunities for the firm to enhance its competitive advantage."[39] If a manufacturing company can tie its suppliers into its inventory and manufacturing information system, the cost of business transactions can be lowered and the CIM concept with Just-In-Time supply arrivals can streamline operations. However, the manufacturer can scan the databases of all suppliers for the lowest prices, effectively putting suppliers at the whim of the manufacturer.

On the other hand, suppliers can increase their leverage by providing customers with new value-added information services and, in the process, raise the cost for customers to switch to a different supplier. American Hospital Supply's use of order entry terminals in customer locations was mentioned earlier as the premier example of supplier power through technology. By providing its customers with the added service of insurance claims processing through its computers, Foremost-McKesson not only increased its share of the pharmaceutical business but also changed the structure of drug wholesaling and increased its customer loyalty.[40]

The ideal solution to buyer-supplier power positioning is joint collaboration. It is possible to benefit both the supplier and the customer by optimizing the performance of activities and the coordination of ordering, shipment, and delivery schedules between the two parties. Porter cites the example of a mutual agreement between a chocolate producer and supplier. "By agreeing to deliver bulk chocolate to a confectionery producer in tank cars instead of solid bars, for example, an industrial chocolate firm saves the cost of molding and packaging while the confectionery manufacturer lowers the cost of in-bound handling and melting."[41] Computer-to-computer linkages between companies allow for such cooperation and optimization.

Customer Satisfaction

When a sales representative makes a sale, a commitment of the entire organization is made. No excuses can be made for sales reps (in any industry) taking an order and then leaving the processing of that order to someone at corporate headquarters. Customers demand and deserve personal attention. To the customer, his or her order is the most important order a sales rep will ever take (no matter that it may be a small order to the seller). Long-term customer confidence and repeat business is founded on a consistent record of doing the little things right and not making the customer feel like merely an order number.

Enter the sales support system. The wealth of information in corporate and regional sales office databases can be made available to sales representatives in the field. With portable computers such as those provided by Hewlett-Packard, Wang, IBM, and Toshiba, sales reps can use telephone lines to connect to the sales, order, inventory, and product marketing databases to prepare for customer calls by reviewing an account profile and tracking customer orders.

Some vendors, like Digital, provide turnkey integrated sales systems applicable to the entire organization. With such a system, remote sales reps can have sales leads and customer inquiries routed to them while a central office simultaneously mails promotional material to the potential customer. Customers see a representative quicker, and the sales rep reduces the number of "cold calls." When a prospect wants further information, the rep can respond quickly to questions about prices, product availability, shipping dates, warranties, and credit status from the customer's site and without playing telephone tag with someone at headquarters. Direct access to inventory data allows sales reps to manage customer commitments, further solidifying customer confidence.

Digital representatives have an added weapon that ensures that correct configurations of complicated *VAXcluster* computers are quoted. An in-house expert system makes decisions on how to configure orders from the more than 10,000 options available.[42]

Selective access to a corporation's sales system by customers may be granted so they can enter routine orders themselves and check the status or shipments directly. Since orders may be submitted quickly, customers have more flexibility and power in actively managing their inventories to lower levels. This has been an important benefit to customers of a large pharmaceutical company.

Here's an example of customer satisfaction as a result of access to the sales database. Westvaco's computer informs customers' computers when shipments have left Westvaco. Customers are provided with a description of large rolls of paper, the paper grade, weight, roll width, and other data. The information is available for customer decision making well in advance of the shipment's arrival.[43]

Portable computer access for sales representatives has been such a windfall in providing customer service that at least one large consumer products company has outfitted its entire sales force with laptop PCs. So has the smaller sales force of Schwinn Bicycle Company. Schwinn has reduced its dealer order turnaround time from nine days to six, thereby boosting sales as the company's information systems director cites in an interview with *Info-systems* magazine. In 1986, 350,000 portables were shipped to dealers, and they are expected to top 1.4 million by 1990.[44]

Better Marketing

Technology can affect the way a firm markets its products and services. Systems that support the sales function can provide higher levels of service to customers, and market segments can be measured more carefully as better data on customers become available.

The integrated sales system, like the one mentioned in the previous section, provides significant benefits to the sales or marketing manager. For example, by tapping into the sales database and applying a sales decision support program, the district manager may review weekly sales by product category, territory, or market segment. Daily monitoring of account activity, shipping schedules, and inventory status ensures against overcommitments. A summary report on lead activity can help in matching personnel resources to types of accounts or sales territories. Account profitability analysis can help reveal the actual cost of servicing accounts, allowing management to decide how to use the sales personnel most effectively. With direct access to sales information, the marketing staff can eliminate guesswork and make forecasts based on real and likely orders.

No industry concentrates on marketing more than the consumer goods giants, such as Procter & Gamble, Colgate-Palmolive, Unilever, Clorox, and Johnson & Johnson. In this relatively stable marketplace, basic consumer goods are purchased regardless of economic conditions. Whether we're rich or unemployed,we need to purchase such items as soap, deodorant, toilet paper, shampoo, diapers, and household cleaning products. Unlike the auto or computer industries that experience wide boom and bust periods based on economic conditions, consumer goods manufacturers compete for greater shares of a market that is fairly predictable. With only 1 to 2 percent growth in the total market, companies cannot rely on riding the coattails of industry growth. On the contrary, consumer goods companies have corporate strategies meant to gain market share by capitalizing on shifting consumer preferences.

Environmental concerns, such as the phosphate restrictions imposed a decade ago, and consumer trends, such as long or short hair, natural foods, and the fitness craze, also play a part in the growth or decline of major product lines. With a detailed knowledge of the consumer, these companies, whose profit margins are measured in pennies per item, wage daily war on the grocery shelves of the United States, Canada, Mexico, South America, Japan, and Western Europe for even a fraction of a share point.

In a mature marketplace, consumer goods companies have found that competitive advantage is gained by changing their approaches to business in ways that generate profits and garner increased market share. There is an ongoing challenge to perform ever-deeper analyses of the marketplace to find new sources of increased volume and operational practices that produce profit. Knowledge of the consumer and the power of persuasion is everything. For example, millions are spent to learn the average number of toothbrush strokes, to find out whether water is applied to the brush before or after the toothpaste, and to measure whether deodorant applied in the morning or at night is more effective. Brand managers and researchers know the intimate details of the life of the "average American" along hundreds of dimensions of demographic variables. (In graduate school, I frequently heard that a couple of years of brand experience at P&G, the dean of consumer goods research, was like getting a Ph.D. in marketing from the best business school.)

Not only do companies like P&G spend heavily on research, they are, beyond doubt, the largest advertisers in America. This is the industry that developed the, appropriately named, "soap opera" to advertise their products to "homemakers." It is also the business that is the basis of most advertising textbooks. Bob Goligoski, writing for *Business Computer Systems*, notes that when a company such as Clorox has annual sales of $1.1 billion of bleach, paint, charcoal briquettes, and salad dressing and spends $137 million on advertising, that company wants to know that that 12 percent of its income is being spent effectively and will produce bottom-line sales.[45]

Brand managers at twenty-five large companies like Clorox, Johnson & Johnson, Pepsico, Carnation, and Beatrice are being joined by companies in other industries such as shipper American President Lines, the brokerage firm Kidder Peabody, and CBS Records and are becoming aware of the power of a computer-based tool as a competitive weapon.[46] They are realizing that the massive volume of raw consumer preference and sales data can provide insight into more effective marketing operations, but to manage all that data would require a large staff or the right computer-based tools. Rather than hiring larger staffs, using intuition, or waiting for months for MIS to run an analysis of the market, these leaders are using a product from Metaphor Computer Systems of Mountain View, California. Metaphor offers a decision support tool that allows the brand manager to monitor the performance of a brand, do market research using internal company records and external databases of product sales, determine product prices and advertising budgets, and better assess how the product will be marketed.

Metaphor is a departmental network of brand management workstations linked to a database server and a compute server that, together, provide the brand manager with an electronic desk and query capability. Queries can be done against databases storing Nielsen's audits of hundreds of products sold in grocery stores, scanner data from ten major markets, and Selling Areas-Marketing Inc. (SAMI) reports on the movement of over 475 product categories in fifty-four markets. Correlations between advertising expenditures and market share increases are quickly provided by *Metaphor* in report or graphical form. Rapid feedback on the effectiveness of advertising in various markets allows consumer goods companies to cut back on ads that have little effect on sales and quickly learn the characteristics of successful ads for possible reapplication by other managers.

"The ability of the *Metaphor* system to quickly convert market research data for analysis shortens Clorox's reaction time to changing market conditions," according to Goligoski.[47] Metaphor users can also learn where and what the competition is advertising, how much is being spent for ads, how effective they are, what coupon promotions are being used, and how they relate to sales results. The system also looks at external databases for things that may affect sales. For example, seasonal sales of charcoal may be affected by weather conditions. With Metaphor, regional weather information can be retrieved and integrated with other data for a better decision based on a broader set of information.

In the highly competitive consumer goods industry, every edge that can be obtained is important. Metaphor provides an edge to the user who makes intelligent marketing moves based on better information. If such information adds to the market share by even one or two points, it could mean millions in profits.

Desktop video is providing another cost-effective alternative for marketing departments. Promotional videos may now be produced in-house, without costly ad agencies and without the graphic arts department. Replacing the 35mm slide presentation is the animated computer graphic presentational videotape made with software for an *IBM PC-AT* and a home video camera. For about $700, Visual Communications Network of Cambridge, Massachusetts, offers a product called *Concorde* that runs on a personal computer and allows unsophisticated users to produce simple graphics and animation.

Targa Systems of Hartford, Connecticut, provides a $15,000 system that combines the most advanced electronic digitizers, sound systems, and graphic devices. Holding the attention of the audience is now a color presentation with dissolving screens, fading titles, and information highlighted with strobe effects. According to *Business Week* reporter Jeffrey Rothfeder, companies like Travelers Insurance are able to replace $250,000 in outside studio services with desktop video promotions illustrating a particular service that may be customized for each client.[48]

Marketing doesn't always have to be for purely profit-making purposes. Not-for-profit organizations also benefit from advanced information systems. According to Carlton Smith of Mitre Corporation, the National Eye Care Project (NECP), a computer-based program for aiding senior citizens with eye care problems, has resulted in over 92,000 patient referrals for conditions like cataracts, refractive errors, and macular degeneration. A toll-free number allows prospective patients to talk with operators who key information into a dedicated *IBM PC* workstation which is connected to the *ICM System/36*. The system provides the operator with guidelines for questioning, and the operator's input is the beginning of a patient record.

Based on the questions, the computer performs a referral match to ophthalmologists in the patient's area. When the patient is near many doctors, the system invokes a load-balancing algorithm to distribute referrals among local physicians. At the same time, mailing labels are printed to send the patient more information on eye disease, and the ophthalmologist's office is informed to expect the patient as a referral. Senior citizens are helped regardless of their ability to pay. The success of the program is measured by the fact that it has brought in 32 percent of patients who, before NECP, never had an eye examination.[49]

Competitor Intelligence

The importance of information to the firm has been constantly stressed throughout this book. Certainly, the impact of information on the value chain underscores this. There is a growing need for internal information derived from operations, but there will continue to be a growing need for information external to the enterprise. Competitor intelligence—too often an informal network of who read or heard the latest rumor—can be systematized with computer-based technology. In addition, the deplorable state of intelligence gathering by most firms, even the largest of the Fortune 500, offers a prime opportunity to the company that gains almost any advantage in this area.

It is not uncommon to see major industry players operate on knowledge that is incomplete, widely scattered throughout the corporation, and generally not coordinated. Information that exists from internal "experts" tends to be in conflict, unsubstantiated on facts, and often based on assumptions and intuitive hunches that are sometimes right, sometimes wrong, and usually out of date.[50]

Online databases provide a solution to this malaise. Sources of competitor intelligence, including industry watchers, trade associations, trade presses, government experts, consultants, financial analysts, public filings, and research studies, can be located and retrieved using computer technology. The general rule of thumb today is that almost any document that is available in print can be found somewhere in electronic form. Because such information is in computer-readable form, companies can use their in-house systems or a subscription service to automatically search millions of documents, analyses, news stories, press releases, SEC filings, and reports to develop a portfolio of what the competition is up to. Because a database is flexible, and because any portion can be scanned, there is little chance that a company name or product will be missed.

However, database searches aren't panaceas. Once the data are retrieved, managers or staff analysts still have to determine the relevancy of particular reports or news stories. But because a computer is persistent, it frequently and reliably examines places that are easily overlooked by humans.

Of course, there is a trade-off between too much information and the assurance of not missing a key piece of information. The last thing a busy manager wants to do is review hundreds of pages of computer printout only to find that most of it is irrelevant. Advances in language parsing, natural languages, artificial intelligence, and database indexing routines are reducing the severity of this problem. New human interface query languages help computers understand just what the requestor means, and artificial intelligence holds the promise of helping computers understand the context of a document. In the long run, this will give managers less information, but more of the right information needed to track their competitors.

Some of the more interesting databases noted by Leonard Fuld, president of Information Data Search, are these:

1. *NEXIS:* a full-text database with news stories, press releases, financial information, government reports, Wall Street analyst reports on specific companies, patent, and legal information.

2. *Adtrack:* an abstract and index of advertisements that appear in 150 consumer magazines.

3. *ABI/Inform:* a business database that indexes feature articles from over 500 business publications. It focuses on management issues and business decisions and is good for locating significant trends within companies and industries.

4. *Arthur D. Little/Online:* an index of market studies and reports offered by this research and consulting firm.

5. *A.M. Best Data Bases:* complete company-specific data by state and product line plus aggregate insurance data.

6. *Datastream:* a financial database on thousands of companies. It has an international scope and includes company financials, stock prices, and country economic indicators.

7. *D&B—Dun's Market Identifiers 10+:* a complete online company listing. Plants, branches, and headquarters information is included.

8. *Disclosure II:* a financial database that contains summaries of 10-K, 10-Q, 8-K, and 20-F corporate SEC filings.[51]

This is by no means an exhaustive list, but a researcher can begin to see the range and depth of information available for computerized searching. Similar reports exist online for scientific, engineering, chemical, petroleum, electronic, and public sector intelligence gathering. Technology assessors need to weigh the value a technology could add to gaining better access to such data and applying it to various elements of the value chain.

Making Better Decisions

Since the firm's infrastructure includes its management processes, technology can be sought to improve decisions that bear on every aspect of the value chain. Decision support systems and supercomputers are paving new territory on (surprise, not the laboratory) Wall Street. Supercomputers in miniature form from makers such as Alliant and Convex provide the flexibility and specialization needed to perform specific decision support tasks such as spotting arbitrage opportunities, automatic trading, and portfolio mix analysis. Using pattern recognition techniques, originally developed for antisubmarine warfare, supercomputers sift through years of historical data in an attempt to spot barely discernible trading patterns that foreshadowed arbitrage opportunities or to predict major shifts in the economy.

Program trading, noted for causing wild swings (as we saw on October 19, 1987) in the stock market, is being reinforced with systems that capture the expertise of successful traders. Linear programming, an established discipline of operations research, is being used to determine the optimum mix of stocks, bonds, and other securities in a portfolio. Reporter John Verity cites with optimism a Securities Industry Association report that computers are now the largest single budget item among Wall Street firms.[52]

Decision support systems are getting easier to use and much more customized for personal decision and thinking styles. Pilot Executive Software offers a software package that runs on IBM mainframes or Digital *VAX* computers and helps managers search for trends and exceptions to parameters of sales or other specified business functions. This in itself isn't earth shattering. MIS analysts have been providing their clients with exception reports for twenty years. What makes Pilot's *Advantage System* stand out is its flexibility. Analysts provide fixed exception reports, for example, and just as they are delivering the finished report, the manager wants to see the data sliced and prepared a different way. Advantage allows the non-technical manager to draft a report and then, with each review, instruct the system to inspect the underlying data in the database until the desired level of detail is reached.

David Friend, chairman of Pilot, notes, "You never know which 1 percent you want each month."[53] Advantage solves this problem by letting the user "drill-down" to lower levels of detail or summarize up to higher levels of exception reporting. When such flexibility is added, managers are more likely to speculate, unconstrained by fixed reports.

Expert systems are being used to extend the knowledge base of valuable human resources and improve the quality of decisions. This is especially important in key business functions where expertise is concentrated among a few individuals or where many complex operations are involved in a process. For example, IBM uses an expert system to advise its field personnel on how to move mainframe computers from site to site.[54] While visiting the Dallas InfoMart in 1983 (a mall devoted to computer vendors), I was pleasantly surprised by the usefulness of a system from Texas Instruments that queried me about my business and its goals and produced a printout of applications and vendors located in the InfoMart that could be important to my business.

A wealth of new artificial intelligence (AI) advisors have been developed for the financial services industry. Syntelligence, of Sunnyvale, California, offers *Lending Advisor* for retail banks and *Underwriting Advisor* for the property/casualty insurance industry.[55] Because an AI system can help the manager evaluate a large number of variables, it can improve decision making by using experience and forcing structure where it was previously nonexistent. For example, when banks make loans, they are actually making decisions on the future cash flows of the firm. For such decisions, there are no absolute answers. It doesn't replace the experience and judgment of loan officers, but it establishes a common level of performance of assets and helps the bankers ask more of the right questions. The system has found favor among BankAmerica Corporation, Wells-Fargo Bank, and First Wachovia Corporation.[56]

The technology that facilitates increases in the effectiveness of financial decision making can be applied with 3-D graphics to also simulate manufacturing plants during the design phase. Northern Research & Engineering, a subsidiary of Ingersoll-Rand, used a simulation system to check the accuracy of a manufacturing line design. Instead of needing seventy-seven tools performing sixteen different operations, as the original design specified, they were able to eliminate four machines from the shop floor. This represented a savings of $750,000 for their client.[57] In the future, we will certainly expect to see these assistants added to existing text retrieval systems, financial modeling, portfolio mix, and manufacturing quality-control applications.

CRITICAL SUCCESS FACTORS

Technology assessment seeks to match enterprise objectives and technical developments, but just how do we know that a technology will contribute to the bottom line? We have shown how information systems can positively affect the efficiency of operations and the effectiveness of exploiting new opportunities, but how can managers feel confident that a group of technologies will be relevant to the goals of the organization? By asking, "In what ways can a proposed technology contribute to the *critical success factors (CSF)* of the firm?" technology assessors have yet another tool to evaluate the appropriateness of applications while bolstering management's confidence in the selection.

CSFs were introduced by John Rockart in a *Harvard Business Review* article in 1979. Since then the method has gained acceptance in a growing number of organizations. CSFs are the limited number of areas in which satisfactory results will ensure successful competitive performance for the individual, department, or for the total organization. They are the few areas where "things must go right" for the business to flourish and for the manager's goals to be attained.[58]

The CSF process is simple, consistent, inexpensive, and can be tailored to the needs of people and departments in any area of the enterprise. CSFs derive from the firm's mission statement. Three to five primary objectives are then identified. The next step is a series of interviews that determine what departmental factors must be successful in order for the prime objectives to be met. The factors are consolidated and simplified to form a reduced, manageable set of CSFs.

Critical measures of these factors are then determined. This helps clearly state to the organization just what defines success and failure. For instance, measures for a data processing operation may be uptime, user response time, application access, and number of users supported. An airline may choose occupied seats, a retail bank may look at the average daily balance of depositors, and a grocery chain may consider stock turnover a critical success factor.

The exact indicator will vary by industry and by company, but the CSFs chosen need to be measurable. When CSFs cannot be measured, subjective indicators, such as customer satisfaction surveys, are useful. From the critical measures, goals for success and bounds for failure are determined. Information systems can then be used to monitor various business statistics that indicate business success or failure as it relates to the CSFs.[59] This process is graphically summarized in Figure 4-9.

CSFs are indicators of the health of the business. Although Rockart developed the method to understand the information requirements of chief executives, Christine Bullen joined Rockart in elaborating on how each organization and individual, from the CEO to the first-line manager can benefit from CSFs. For example, if the CEO and top management team develop corporate CSFs, it is incumbent on each subordinate department to use a similar process to determine how they may contribute to the CSFs of the company. In turn, individuals use the method to develop their own CSFs that show how they might contribute directly to the CSFs of the department.

In terms of the information systems strategy, CSFs have a one-to-one relationship to the objectives of the individual, department, and organization. This is so because the CSFs define critical areas of the business that must be monitored and controlled. Managers responsible for these critical areas need, by definition, sufficient information to determine whether events are proceeding well in each area. Information is religiously collected relating to the CSFs, and computerized exception reports are produced. Such reporting is straightforward and highlights when CSF indicators fall outside acceptable limits. From this perspective, CSFs can be used with information systems to increase the efficiency of business operations. In this case, CSFs are used to gauge the performance of financial control systems, inventory management, distribution routing, and management information systems that report business activities.

On the other hand, because CSFs are linked to the critical areas where failure is not allowed, they point out key areas where information systems might expand opportunities—what we have defined in this text as strategic computing. In other words, if a technology can be expected to produce substantial benefits in CSF areas, then it is likely that it should be added to the technology portfolio of the firm (even if its benefits are quite intangible). This could lead to investments in decision support or expert systems that advise managers on effective use of advertising expenditures or the feasibility

Figure 4-9
The Critical Success Factors Process

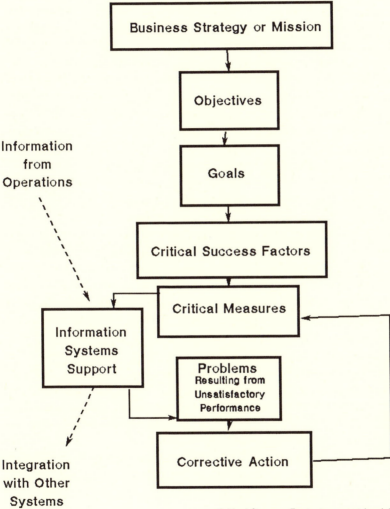

Business Strategy or Mission

Objectives

Goals

Critical Success Factors

Critical Measures

Information
from
Operations

Information
Systems
Support

Problems
Resulting from
Unsatisfactory
Performance

Corrective Action

Integration
with Other
Systems

Critical Success Factors concept by John F. Rockart,
MIT Center for Information Systems Research.
Adapted and presented by Strategic Systems
with permission.

of acquisitions via "what-if" questioning, for example. In fact, John Sviokla, writing for the Association for Computing Machinery's (ACM) journal, *Data Base*, reports that Digital Equipment is creating an expert system to screen volumes of quality data and judge their content.[60] It directly supports quality improvement—a CSF for Digital. Thus, almost any task which directly supports a CSF is desirable, according to Sviokla.

Critical success factors provide significant benefits to the implementing organization. Taking the time to think through and record CSFs allows management to focus on the key problems and opportunities of the business. It also provides a means of hierarchical communication by executives to departments as to what is really important and provides a clear definition of the amount and kind of information that must be collected.

The process also limits the costly collection and reporting of data to what is absolutely necessary. CSFs prevent MIS departments from falling into the trap of collecting and reporting the information that happens to be easy to collect. Rather, it focuses attention on data that might not otherwise be collected but are key for the success of the particular department or manager involved.[61] The same can be said for application systems and technologies. Without CSFs, MIS might tend to constantly use the technology at its disposal. CSFs point systems expenditures to those crucial areas of the business that must be successful, which can have the effect of stretching MIS staffs beyond their conventional scope to force a search for innovative systems and technologies that support efforts in CSF areas.

For the technology assessor, there are also significant benefits to be gained by a CSF exercise, including greater insight into the business and establishment of a set of priorities that allows for increased consulting effectiveness.

COST JUSTIFICATION

I have repeatedly stated throughout this book that technology cannot be implemented for technology's sake. Rational business judgment must prevail. As such, once a particular technology is chosen as a potential solution to an actual business problem or once the technology is expected to open new business opportunities, cost justification becomes an issue.

Cost justification is a common practice used to determine whether or not expenditures for a piece of capital equipment will be offset by the revenue generated by that equipment. It is a form of cost-benefit analysis that has also been extended to decisions regarding information systems acquisitions. However, it is SSI's contention that information systems technology is different from other kinds of capital equipment. Where justifying the worth of a drill press in a machine shop relates to the productivity of labor, measuring the value of today's information systems is more difficult because it involves an assignment of worth on knowledge worker productivity.

Computer technology also involves a judgment as to the value of information to the firm—a subjective task at best. As an enabling technology that has the potential to go beyond cost-reduction efficiencies to opening up new business possibilities, it has no precedent. Since computers and their subsequent applications are changing the way we work and the way we look at work, the well-defined rules of cost justification, appropriate for a turn-of-the-century steel plant, are not entirely appropriate for this new technology.

Information technology is different from other technologies commonly justified by an enterprise; therefore, our approach to cost justification must also be different. We agree with Wang Laboratories' view that cost justifying information systems technology is a complex issue that involves judgments of worth based on different technologies, different users, applications, business types, industry structures, and different user levels of technological experience.[62] (Wang's booklet entitled *Cost Justification* is an excellent primer on the subject.) There can be no one method of justification. Rather, there are combinations of approaches, each with a unique blend of influences.

It is not my intent to offer a cookbook approach to cost justification. Rather, the following five points are considerations designed to guide the technology assessor in understanding the cost-benefit issues that influence technology selection and approval processes.

Cost Displacement

Cost displacement refers to the actual dollar savings the firm is expected to realize as a result of implementing a particular technology. This is the approach to cost justification most commonly understood by managers. It grew out of the industrial revolution and is best used when deciding to automate repetitive work. In factories, a robot spot welder controlled by a minicomputer could replace five human welders or do the same job in one-fifth the time. In the office, a word processing system could allow more documents to be typed and edited displacing several typewriters and allowing some of the typists to be reassigned to other, more fulfilling work. Courier costs could be eliminated by the use of fax machines, electronic mail, and remote job entry stations connected from remote offices to corporate headquarters over telecommunications lines. Cost displacement is the easiest type of cost-benefit analysis because it allows the comparison of tangible assets and measurable results in the current mode of operation to the same variables under the proposed system.

Cost Avoidance

Related to cost displacement is cost avoidance. Also a comparison of tangible results to "hard dollar" expenses, cost avoidance refers to the elimination of future spending, and it can be seen as the flip side of cost displacement. In this case, an information system is expected to do more work in either the same or less time.

A good example is the telephone company's use of automatic table look-up systems. In the good old days, operators would assist callers in finding a phone number or an address. In today's post-breakup environment, local phone companies needed a means to meet growing customer requests for subscriber information while keeping a tight rein on costs. Enter the computer database, interactive query languages, and voice synthesizers. By integrating these technologies, a smaller number of operators can support more customers, delegating the most time-consuming tasks to the system— searching subscriber listings and relaying the telephone number to the caller in an electronic voice. Although some of the personal touch is gone, local phone companies have been able to defer the need to add more clerical staff, keep their costs low, and compete in an industry that is price-sensitive.

Added Value

A more controversial method of cost justification is the added-value approach. It involves a subjective judgment that seeks to qualify, rather than quantify, the benefits gained from having more of the right information at the right time. Added-value benefits include such things as having access to information that was previously unavailable. Such information could dramatically affect stock purchase, loan approval, plant location, or advertising placement decisions. The outcome of such decisions are difficult to measure until after the fact, and they involve two kinds of risk—the risk of losing investments if the wrong decision is made, and the risk of losing opportunity for returns if no action is taken.

So technologies that can help give better customer service, improve the quality of managers' decisions, and hasten time-to-market of new products can be justified by the subjective added-value approach. One can think of the added-value approach as analogous to employee training: Few tangible dollars can be traced to it, but every company must train their employees as a long-term investment in their abilities to effectively perform their assignments. Also, the subjective impact on employee job enrichment is another area that cannot be underestimated.

Ultimately, like training, added-value investments in computer technology can derive (and is expected to produce) tangible returns, but managers must be willing to accept a degree of risk. Technology assessors can help managers justify the associated risk by asking, "What dollar amount would you be willing to pay for this computer capability if it allowed your firm to do X additional tasks or improve by a factor of Y on the effectiveness of those tasks currently being done?"

Technology Imperative

In today's competitive environment, companies that adopt technology after their competitors already have find that technical projects can be easily justified as a matter of survival. Citing technology imperative, late adopters have a sense of urgency that stems from answering "no" to the question: "Can the firm afford to be without this capability?"

The American auto industry's late adoption of robotics is an example of this method of cost justification. When faced with the realization that their ability to compete on quality and price was directly related to their successful implementation of automated factories, the "Big Three" made the justification of major robotics projects an effortless task for technology assessors. The same could be said of banks that waited until market share was permanently lost before they adopted automatic teller machines. Today, no major bank can compete as a credible service business without ATMs.

Waiting until a technology proves itself causes businesses to risk falling behind industry leaders. This realization has led to the general acceptance of a more subjective approach to cost justification.

Strategic Opportunity

Strategic opportunity is an entrepreneurial approach to cost justification that is gaining favor as technology opens up new business potential. Story after story is told of how early adopters of a technology use it as a strategic weapon over the competition. Clearly a risky proposition and involving the most subjective of judgments, the strategic opportunity approach is an amplified version of the added-value approach. The differences are a matter of magnitude.

Companies that use strategic opportunity ask questions such as: "How will the trends in information technology impact our markets, products, and services?" "What value do we assign to being able to exploit these trends?" "Where will we be in five years if we don't accept this technology now?" These questions and their answers tend to involve the highest levels of management, involve larger projects, and can set the entire enterprise down a course of no return.

As an example, consider again the case of American Airlines' SABRE system. On a pure cost-benefit basis, we doubt that the system could have displaced enough clerks or reduced enough paperwork to justify its massive development costs. But visionary management allowed SABRE to be justified based on American's ability to lock travel agents into a nationwide interactive system that displayed American's flights first. The market share gained in the early years of the system's operation more than exceeded the multimillion-dollar development costs.

SYSTEMS INTEGRATION

After the technology assessment consultant has (1) considered corporate objectives, (2) envisioned the future, (3) examined potentially relevant technologies, (4) judged whether a technology can improve the cost or differentiation position of the firm, and (5) determined the range of financially feasible alternatives available, systems integration needs to be considered. By systems integration, we mean the degree to which a technology can be easily connected and operated in a way that leverages the firm's existing computing investment and simultaneously provides the benefits to the value chain expected by the firm. In simple terms, the technology must fit the current environment or provide enough incentive for the firm to change the environment.

Some of the most classic technology battles in the corporation are likely to occur between the MIS department (charged with improving efficiency) and the systems developers (charged with helping line managers improve the profit and loss position of their departments). MIS may have spent decades building a reliable computing monolith stored away in a controlled environment. This mainframe keeps the business running. Corporate production systems, such as payroll, order processing, inventory status, and accounts receivable, are sacred in this environment, and new technologies impose a risk to the efficiency of this "glass-house" operation. The systems developer, consultant, or technology assessor, by proposing a new solution that changes the way the firm operates, may find extreme resistance to an untried technology. Concerns by MIS on the technology's supportability and its risk to the established environment are real and valid.

As part of facilitating the integration process and reducing MIS's concerns, technology assessors need to at least consider the management and technical issues raised by the following questions:

1. How will the new system communicate with current systems? If they don't communicate, are gateway products available to bridge the communications gap? Does it merely connect via cables, or can it go beyond connectivity to share files, allow programs on the mainframe to call programs on the new system (and vice versa), and is it manageable by the central staff? Do the communications protocols conform to international standards, de facto industry standards, or some non-standard? Does the implementation require installation of new wiring?

   A good example of this problem can be seen as minicomputer and workstation vendors seek to conform to the international networking standards while mainframe vendors have enough clout to push their own networks (e.g., IBM's *Systems Network Architecture* or *SNA*). Although, some of the most creative end-user applications come from smaller vendors, there remains a need to conform to the de facto IBM SNA standard. Small computer manufacturers face a dilemma: Do they stress their unique benefits that may build on a non-SNA standard, or do they conform to SNA, whether it complements their products or not? Ultimately there must be a trade-off. This dichotomy has opened the market for networking devices that translate between these diverse protocols.

2. What are the file formats? Are they standard or proprietary to the new technology's manufacturer? Can they be accessed by other systems? If not, are database conversion/translator utilities available? For example, will the selection of a database access method conform to standards so that future optical disk products can be used?

3. What data access requirements could conflict with current security regulations? Who "owns" the data stored in the system—a manager or department or is it a corporate resource? How will access be controlled?

4. Does the new technology require a large training effort by the support personnel, or are similar technologies currently in use? For example, new operating systems can require significant training.

5. Does the new technology require a specialized physical environment, or can it physically coexist in the same facility as the firm's existing computers? Supercomputers, for example, might require specialized cooling equipment.

6. Will the new technology be accessible via desktop workstations? If those workstations are personal computers, are they restricted to a particular type or vendor's model(s)?

7. What is the long-term impact on the firm's technology strategy and selection alternatives as a result of choosing this technology now? Does it allow for flexible modifications as the company's business changes, or does it build a chain of events that preclude changing without major losses of the firm's investment?

8. Does the new technology allow itself to be leveraged across the current implementing department to future unforeseen technologies in other areas of the business?

9. Are there any special restrictions imposed by government agencies that would keep the firm from realizing its full investment in this technology? In Europe there are very diverse and restrictive laws plus high tariffs for certain kinds of transborder data flow. To what extent would this affect plans to link up and share information among offices of a multinational company, for example?

CONSIDER THE USER

Perhaps the most important consideration in analyzing a new technology's applicability is this: Consider how people with non-technical backgrounds will use a new technology as a tool. The technology cannot be the master, and technology assessors should never allow themselves to become "technically competent barbarians." They must always consider the human element. This sounds so simple that it is almost trite. After all, user friendliness is what every computer company strives for, right? Well, my colleagues and I have found that this message cannot be overstated. Because the designers of technical products typically have a different worldview than the product's users, engineers too often take for granted that "everyone knows this, so why write it down" or "users won't mind hitting these three keys at the same time; we do it in the lab all the time." They often have a hard time understanding that most users don't exist in the world of the design lab and, as such, don't have or want the skill set of a group of engineers. Complicated operations that seem simple to design engineers must still be reduced to hitting a single button for 90 percent of the users of a technical product.

Programmers certainly need an in-depth technical education, and we advocate a broadening of this technical base with humanistic values and experiences. But the most important thing for technology assessors (who probably have a firm grounding in one or more technologies) to remember is that the rest of the organization will be computer users, not programmers. They will not have, nor should they be expected to acquire, programming skills. People use computers with confidence as just another tool to help them perform their jobs. They expect to use computers as secondary tools, just as they use telephones, calculators, and typewriters. They are articulate and literate, but they should not have to be technically sophisticated to use a business tool.

Some of the most interesting and advanced work in the field of user acceptance of computers is being done at the Aetna Life & Casualty Company. The firm has formed a People/Technology Programs unit that is dedicated to assessing the impact of technology on people. Aetna stresses the adoption of systems that are *Normal to Use*.[63] Normal-to-Use systems differ from the familiar terms of *easy to use* and *user friendly*. Easy-to-use systems may not be easy to learn, and user friendly systems may be easy to learn but difficult to use. For example, Richard Telesca, an Aetna consultant, notes how an easy-to-use system for experienced users may involve multiple key combinations or special codes that make operations quicker. Yet these keys and codes are not usually standard business operations and must be committed to memory over time. On the other hand, user friendly software that is easy to learn usually incorporates extensive menu systems. "Menus, while important for the novice, can become cumbersome and annoying to the experienced operator if alternate means of system navigation is not provided," according to Telesca. Contrast these common system approaches with Aetna's Normal-to-Use systems.

Normal-to-Use describes the system's temperament. It incorporates the language and procedures that are familiar to workers and terminology that is part of a given business function. Learning the system is easy because it is designed along business lines using intellectual procedures with which workers are comfortable. "Learning and use becomes almost intuitive," says Telesca. The system's screens, messages, and operational procedures are more effective when expressed in the language of the user and when they follow the business procedures familiar to users. The normal use system may not be the easiest to use, but it is the most effective for its particular operator.

Technology assessors need to shake off that old "hacker" stereotype and incorporate the Normal-to-Use concepts in their selection of technologies for business applications. Elements to consider, according to Telesca, are these:

- A *menu system* that offers advantages to the novice user because user training is minimal but also offers a list of selection dialogues, optional overrides, and command languages for the more experienced user. The menu should use the terminology of the industry of the user and could ideally be modified by the user for his or her company's jargon.

- *Good screen design* concepts that display relevant information for the user's task in a format and layout that is most productive to the user. Colors, in some instances, simplify use. For example, use red for overdrawn accounts or errors. Symbols, icons, and other graphics that are natural to the operator's experience base may allow the operator to recognize options and procedures quicker and easier than text would.

- *Consistency in operation* between systems is important to allow the transfer of experience from one application to another. Whenever possible, the same result should occur every time a particular key is depressed. If color is used, it must be used consistently to provide interpretation of messages and for easy use for those who are color blind, for users with tinted glasses, and to account for the occasion where an application may be used on a monochromatic terminal.

- *The dialogue* should be in the vocabulary of the users. Systems menus, data entry, and inquiry screens should be expressed in simple terms that are relevant to the user. Computer jargon and mnemonics should be avoided to reduce training and possible confusion.

- *Prefill input fields* with data when possible. The operator should not have to input data the system already "knows." For example, insurance systems should allow operators to enter a policy number; the system then completes the insured's name, address, and other constant data. There should be no reason to ask extra work of the user when the system has this information stored, yet available.

- *Special function keys* can be set up to perform a specific task with a keystroke, by pointing an electronic wand, or by touching the screen. However, the purpose of each key should be clear to the user (almost intuitive).

- *An indication of what the system is doing* prevents the operator from having to stare at a blank screen while the computer is processing work. It also keeps users from mistaking background computer processing for poor system response, and it allows the user to decide whether other human work can be performed while the system is processing.

- *Interrupt/resume functions* are similar to the "hold" button on the telephone. Users can interrupt their work to access data through a different system or perform an intermediate function. Having done so, users can return to their original operation without having lost their place or data. Natural breaks should be provided in the application, such as when a form is completed, to reduce stress and errors.

- *Error correction* should be as easy to perform as making the original mistake. Error messages should make sense to the user and provide some indication of how to correct the problem where possible. Erroneous data should be highlighted. "Undo" or "backup" commands and "help" facilities need to be standard features of a Normal-to-Use system.

TECHNOLOGY ASSESSMENT IN PERSPECTIVE

Admittedly, these technology assessment considerations are not really rules but are examples of what works for us at Strategic Systems. No earth-shattering new computer buzzwords or revolutionary academic concepts are revealed. However, the value of our approach lies in how proven business concepts promoted by noted researchers can be synthesized into a managerial framework for decision making on computer technology selection (see Figure 4-10). Also of importance to us is how the SSI process fosters an understanding of the range of new technologies at the manager's disposal and their potential competitive applications through systems integration.

Although we have used many computer- and communications-based applications as examples, it is our assertion that *technology assessment*, as an approach to problems, is also valid for a broader range of technologies. Advanced superconducting materials, space industrialization, alternative energy sources, molecular engineering, and bioengineering are examples of multidisciplinary technologies that are certain to influence the competitiveness of corporations in the future. We encourage readers to consider developments in these areas and how technology assessment may be used to integrate diverse technologies into unique solutions for a broader range of business endeavors.

Fundamentally, technology assessment is not some new magic practiced by technical specialists. Rather, it is a managerial guide and a structured approach embodying common sense. It provides a means to stay competitive by opening up new opportunities and by improving current operations. At

Figure 4-10
The Strategic Systems Model of Technology Assessment

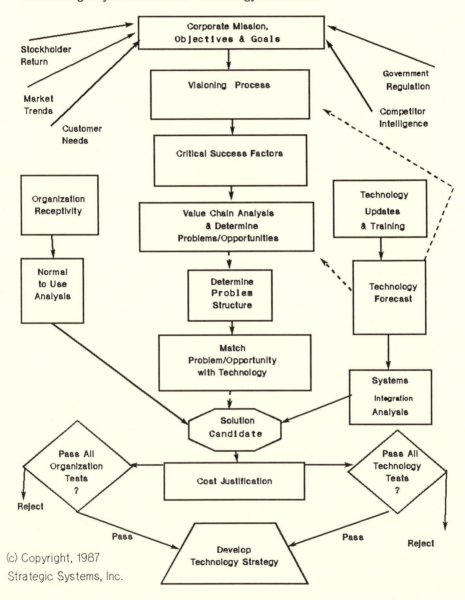

Strategic Systems we believe that competitive success in a highly competitive world demands doing common things in an uncommon manner with the best tools and the most creative techniques. We hope the process described here contributes to this kind of management framework.

NOTES

1. Theodore Levitt, "Marketing Myopia," *Harvard Business Review* (1960), reprinted (September-October 1975), pp. 1-12.

2. Curtis W. Page and Charles Selden, *Asking "Just Right" Business Questions* (New York: Crown Publishers, 1987), pp. 16-17.

3. Levitt, "Marketing Myopia," p. 1.

4. Slogan from 1986 Ford Motor Company advertising campaign.

5. Thomas J. Peters and Robert H. Waterman, *In Search of Excellence* (New York: Harper & Row, 1982), p. 105.

6. Page and Selden, *Asking "Just Right" Business Questions*, p. 17.

7. Richard N. Foster, *Innovation: The Attacker's Advantage* (New York: Summit Books, 1986), p. 31.

8. Ibid., p. 106.

9. Ibid., p. 212.

10. Ibid., pp. 214-17.

11. John J. Sviokla, "Business Implications of Knowledge-Based Systems," *Data Base* (Association for Computing Machinery, Summer 1986), p. 7.

12. Michael E. Porter, *Competitive Advantage: Creating and Sustaining Superior Performance* (New York: The Free Press, 1985), pp. 33-200.

13. Michael E. Porter and Victor E. Millar, "How Information Gives You Competitive Advantage," *Harvard Business Review* (July-August 1985), pp. 149-159.

14. Porter, *Competitive Advantage*, pp. 171-176.

15. International Data Corporation, "Factory of the Future," special report (1984).

16. J.M. Kallis, L.A. Strattan, and T.T. Bui, "Program Helps Spot Hot Spots," *IEEE Spectrum* (Institute of Electrical and Electronic Engineers, March 1987), pp. 36-41.

17. Bro Uttal, "Speeding New Ideas to Market," *Fortune* (March 2, 1987), p. 64.

18. Robert B. Mills, "Building a Strategy for CIM,"*CAE* (October 1986), p. 58.

19. Nhora Cortes-Comerer, "JIT Is Made to Order," *IEEE Spectrum* (Institute of Electrical and Electronic Engineers, September 1986), p. 59.

20. Ibid., pp. 57-62.

21. Brad Whitworth, "Cramming Computers with Common Sense," *Measure* (Hewlett-Packard, September-October 1986), p. 3.

22. Cortes-Comerer, "JIT Is Made to Order," p. 57.

23. Ibid.

24. David M. Rappaport, "Voice Mail: Key Tool or Costly Toy?" *Data Communications* (October 1986), p. 153.

25. Lisa Spiegelman, "PC Users Are Taking to Electronic Mail Too Well," *Info-World* (February 16, 1987), p. 17.

26. Ira Monarch and Jaime Carbonell, "CoalSORT: A Knowledge-Based Interface," *IEEE Expert* (Institute of Electrical and Electronic Engineers, Spring 1987), pp. 39-53.

27. *Computerworld* (April 27, 1987).

28. John Gantz, "Will Desktop Publishing Turn Out to Be a Mirage," *InfoWorld* (February 16, 1987), p. 31.

29. "Slide-Making System Delivers Cost Break," *Electronics* (November 27, 1986), p. 95.

30. Jonathan Morell and James Leemon, "Assessment of an Effort to Integrate Computer Functions in an Engineering Design Firm," *Data Base* (Special Interest Group on Business Data Processing of the Association for Computing Machinery, Winter 1987), pp. 17-21.

31. John Eckhouse, "Fax Market Booming in US," *San Francisco Chronicle* (March 2, 1987), p. 31.

32. Ibid.

33. "Handwritten; Machine Read," *Infosystems* (October 1986), p. 41.

34. Michael Lawson, "New Option for Satellite Data Transmission: Shared-Hub Service," *Data Communications* (March 1987), pp. 76-80.

35. Thomas J. Allen, "Organizational Structure, Information Technology, and R&D Productivity," *IEEE Transactions on Engineering Management* (Institute of Electrical and Electronic Engineers, November 1986), pp. 212-17.

36. Digital Equipment Corporation's advertising campaign (1986) in which Avon endorsed DEC's networking products.

37. Jan Snyders, "Making the Mainframe Connection," *Infosystems* (May 1987), p. 36.

38. "An Information Center with Clout," *Infosystems* (October 1986), p. 20.

39. Porter, *Competitive Advantage*, p. 51.

40. William R. King, "Information as a Strategic Resource" (editor's comment), *Management Informations Systems Quarterly* (No. 1, 1983).

41. Porter, *Competitive Advantage*, p. 51.

42. Whitworth, "Cramming Computers with Common Sense," p. 5.

43. Gerard Learmonth and Blake Ives, "Information System Technology Can Improve Customer Service," *Data Base* (Special Interest Group on Business Data Processing of the Association for Computing Machinery, Winter 1987), p. 6.

44. David H. Freedman, "Pushing Computers Out the Door," *Infosystems* (March 1987), pp. 30-32.

45. Bob Goligoski, "Brand Leaders," *Business Computer Systems* (June 1986), pp. 27-33.

46. Ibid., p. 32.

47. Ibid.

48. Jeffrey Rothfeder, "Now Playing at an Office Near You—Desktop Videos," *Business Week* (June 1, 1987), pp. 85-87.

49. Carlton L. Smith, "With an Eye Toward Integration," *Infosystems* (January 1987), pp. 44-45.

50. William L. Sammon, Mark A. Kurland, and Robert Spitalnic, eds., *Competitor Intelligence: An Organizational Framework for Business, Business Competition Intelligence* (New York: John Wiley & Sons, 1984), p. 62.

51. Leonard M. Fuld, *Competitor Intelligence: How to Get It, How to Use It* (New York: John Wiley & Sons, 1985), pp. 227-47.

52. John Verity, "Street Smarts: The Supercomputer Becomes Stock Strategist," *Business Week* (June 1, 1987), p. 84.

53. Charles Babcock, "Pilot Package Lets Executives Drill for Detail," *Computerworld* (May 11, 1987).

54. Whitworth, "Cramming Computers with Common Sense," p. 5.

55. Clinton Wilder, "BankAmerica Cozies Up to AI to Assist Lending Procedure," *Computerworld* (1987).

56. Ibid.

57. William G. Wild and Otis Port, "This Video 'Game' Is Saving Manufacturers Millions," *Business Week* (August 17, 1987), pp. 82-84.

58. Christine V. Bullen and John F. Rockart, "A Primer on Critical Success Factors," *The Rise of Managerial Computing: The Best of the Center for Information Systems Research, Sloan School of Management, Massachusetts Institute of Technology* (Homewood, Ill.: Dow Jones-Irwin), p. 385.

59. John F. Rockart and Adam Crescenzi, "Engaging Top Management in Information Technology," *Sloan Management Review* (Vol. 25, No. 4, 1984), pp. 3-16.

60. Sviokla, "Business Implications of Knowledge-Based Systems," p. 11.

61. John F. Rockart, "Chief Executives Define Their Own Data Needs," *Harvard Business Review* (March-April 1979).

62. Wang Laboratories, "Issues in Information Processing: Cost Justification" (Customer education literature, 1985).

63. Richard J. Telesca, "Principles of a Normal to Use System," *DPMA Newsletter* (Data Processing Management Association, October 1983).

5

It Will Take More than Technology

It makes no sense to employ new technologies and yet operate under the assumptions of the old social system. Although the Bureau of Labor Statistics estimates that, largely due to new technology, productivity will increase at an average rate of 1.7 percent through the mid-1990s, about double the rate of the past ten years, these gains cannot be realized without the support of creative and motivated people.[1]

There is a renewed emphasis on the importance of people, their creative talents, and individual contributions to corporate goals. A decade or so ago, when American companies seemed to operate in a predictable world, it was easier to ask employees to fit into the "system" and to assume that the "system," rather than the people, was responsible for the firm's success, according to sociologist Rosabeth Moss Kanter.[2] She notes, "Only when an organization exists in stable circumstances, when its operations resemble clockwork, unvarying in their practices, can individuals be taken for granted or ignored without peril."

But as world events and competitive pressures—inflation, oil supply fluctuations, monetary devaluations, international politics, and foreign competition—disturb the stability of the business environment, the number of exceptions to corporate executives' assumptions increases. Since a routine response from corporate headquarters can be untimely and ineffective in a dynamic environment, companies are delegating responsibility and turning to their people to make decisions locally. In addition, as Kanter explains, "Individuals actually need to count for more, because it is people within the organization who come up with new ideas. . . . Innovations, whether in products, market strategies, technological processes, or work practices, are designed not by machines but by people."[3]

Kanter's 1981 research solidified her pro-people argument by showing that the twenty-year financial performance of firms with reputations for progressive human resource practices far surpassed the long-term profitability and growth of their counterparts.[4] Because people are the most influential factors in the success or failure of a business enterprise, we at Strategic Systems believe the solution to America's fading competitiveness, sluggish growth, and poor quality cannot be found in a magical "black box" or "quick fix" of the latest technological gadget. Indeed, the way work is organized and managed needs to be revolutionized. The Japanese discovered the importance of human factors years ago, and it, no doubt, is part of their tremendous industrial success. To realize the full potential of automation and information systems, progressive American companies are also integrating workers and technologies.

This chapter discusses several of the humanistic aspects that must be considered for successful technology assessment projects. I start by taking a close look at our profession and its shortcomings because technology assessors must be keenly aware that it will take more than technology to move a business ahead.

HACKERS, NERDS, AND ENTREPRENEURS

I have talked at length throughout this book about the need for user-friendly (or normal-to-use) systems. However, it is clear that user-friendly business tools require user-friendly designers. As engineers, our profession too often forgets this rule. We are sometimes justifiably seen, as Sherry Turkle depicts in *The Second Self*, as stereotypical computer hackers or as lonely scientists who seem out of touch with the needs and shortcomings of humans.[5] She describes their world and their actions as

a culture of people who have grown up thinking of themselves as different, apart, and who have a commitment to what one hacker described as "an ethic of total toleration for anything [that] in the real world would be considered strange." . . . They are in a means-end relationship with the computer. . . . The hackers are always trying to "improve" the system. This can make the system less reliable as a tool for getting things done, because it is always changing. The hackers also make the system more complex, more "elegant" according to their aesthetic, which often makes it more difficult for other people to use. They have a cult of prowess that defines itself in terms of winning over more complex systems.[6]

It is their high level of skill that makes hackers valuable to businesses that are trying desperately to employ technology for bottom-line results. On the other hand, it is their limited exposure to the real world that can offset the very skills they bring to the corporate table. The hacker may be a term defined in the seventies, but the problem of integrating high technology and its devotees into traditional American industries is not new.

In the early days of data processing, managers hired computer specialists to tend the machines and write programs that produced business reports. The programmers of the 1950s came from a myriad of disciplines. They were mathematicians, physicists, musicians, philosophers, and teachers. No criteria existed for their selection. As William Harrison, an engineering manager for Siemens Information Systems, notes, "The selection process came down to: find someone who likes to program, and we will see if they are any good at it."[7] Managers believed that programming would never develop into a profession—certainly not an engineering profession—and universities were not expected to offer formal degree programs in computer science.

At the same time, the demand for software "professionals" increased beyond any rational business forecast. "While professions like mechanical engineering and architecture evolved over hundreds, if not thousands, of years, software engineering was pressured to mature into a profession in less than a decade," according to Harrison. So began software engineering, commonly thought of as merely computer programming. The field developed as a specialty, often seen by business leaders as a cross between science and magic.

Programmers were hired for their special skills and were not expected to contribute in broader business functions. This isolation from the mainstream business environment may have fostered a sorely needed technical support group among the new software professionals, but it also limited their vision and their careers. Historically, software development groups in industrial enterprises were staff organizations that provided an information utility. They responded to the needs of line managers and either were not asked or did not assert a desire to contribute to the business as managers. Although this is certainly not the case in modern industry, thirty years' of software engineers restricted in an organizational niche created in many executives' minds the caricature of the computer hacker or nerd.

Admittedly, this is a gross generalization. But software professionals have often failed to understand, or even tried to understand, the needs of the business managers they served. Unfortunately, such categorizations point out an all-too-common experience of line managers, reinforced by many engineers.

The formation of a "hacker mindset" starts early. Computer devotees may be found glaring at screens with fingers blazing away on a keyboard from college computer centers to junior high school learning labs to elementary students' bedrooms. Such enthusiasm for a skill set that has become an economic necessity is admirable among young people. We at Strategic Systems encourage it. However, we are equally concerned about those people who overemphasize the artificial world of computers or who lose touch with society's broader issues. For example, young computer hackers reveled at their accomplishments in the early- to mid-1980s: breaking into the databanks of the Los Alamos nuclear facility, attempting access to NASA's computers, perusing the patient records of the Sloan-Kettering Cancer Institute, or looking at TRW's credit records of 90 million American consumers. Such behavior is unacceptable from anyone, regardless of age. They are as criminal as the street thug, and their actions might have caused personal damage on an unparalleled scale.

We are left with the impression that their technical education, as well as their home environment, has lacked a humanizing and civilizing thrust. When hackers start out with flagrant disregard for the impact of their use of technology on human lives, we sympathize with the business executive who asserts, "We had better not leave the future of the organization in their hands." In fact, they ignore the most fundamental aspect of data, according to Margie Wells-Davis. She notes, "There are people's life experiences in data. When hackers lack respect for others as persons, they may misunderstand the true significance of what the data represents."[8]

In college, we may find the hacker as a somewhat odd person who frequently prefers the company of machines to humans. Sometimes spending as much as forty-eight sleepless hours in university computer centers coast-to-coast, hackers prefer beating, crashing, and perfecting computer systems to meals, sleep, dating, or good grades. Hackers walk the line between humans and machines. They have given their lives to computers and, in return, gained mastery over it. Their object is to master the technology, not relate to others.

When hackers leave the university setting for the pragmatic industrial world, the most talented and most specialized computer scientists and electrical engineers may go to work for a company whose business is technology production. Silicon Valley in California, Route 128 outside Boston, Research Triangle in North Carolina, The Beltway surrounding Washington, D.C., and similar high-tech havens such as Austin, Texas, become home for the best technologists in America. At these companies, hackers must adapt to deadlines, the competitive business environment, and a semblance of corporate America. But, for the most part, high-tech firms are companies of engineers run by engineers. This environment is conducive to hackers, and they tend to thrive in a small technological niche.

In the Silicon Valleys of America, hackers can continue a lifestyle and a work style similar to their college experience. Long hours and casual dress complement the casual human interactions. As Everett Rogers of Stanford and Judith Larsen of Cognos Associates note in their history of Silicon Valley entitled *Silicon Valley Fever: Growth of High-Technology Culture*, "If the work ethic that dominates high-tech industry is a model for the future, serious issues with far reaching implications are raised."[9] They note how young engineers seem to get a macho thrill by working long days and all weekend. Quoting one engineer who worked fifty-nine days in a row, with the shortest day being eight hours and the longest seventeen, Rogers and Larsen describe a culture that has "an unusually large number of people who sit at a terminal writing computer code for ten hours [and who] are in love with their computer. This may be only one of many factors that explain why the divorce rate in Silicon Valley is even higher than the rate for California as a whole, and California's rate is 20 percent above the US average."

The children of hackers are also special. Although one Silicon Valley school district with 12,000 students has more than 500 children with IQs greater than 145 (a rate about forty times the national average), a 1981 survey showed that one out of eight teenagers in Silicon Valley has a drinking problem.[10]

Rogers and Larsen forewarn of the consequences of the hacker mentality:

> Meritocracy is a positive side of the Silicon Valley work ethic: The single important criterion in determining success is work performance. But there is a sinister side to the work ethic—one is left with few resources and little self-esteem when one's job is pulled away. The same forces that combined to produce the microelectronics industry, highlighted as the shining example of American innovation and entrepreneurial success, also can produce work-obsessed technocrats with a limited life experience and a stunted human understanding.[11]

Many high-tech manufacturers actively seek former hackers because of their specialized skills and because they don't demand much beyond intellectual stimulation and a flexible work environment. The best of them succeed in the Silicon Valleys of America. The others find themselves trying to force fit their approach to life and work in the Fortune 500's traditional industries. These non-technical companies stress manufacturing, sales, marketing, distribution, and finance. Here technology is often seen at best as a useful tool, at worst as a necessary evil needed to keep the firm competitive. The hacker mentality seldom survives the hierarchical structure of these companies. Buried in the MIS department, the hacker becomes either a valued technical professional in a focused area or a tolerated technocrat who is indispensable to the support of a critical corporate application like payroll or shipping orders. Here the hacker mentality is forced to change. A business perspective is demanded, or severe constraints are placed on one's career.

Thinking patterns and assumptions that are appropriate for computers can often make it difficult for hackers to interact with people. Approaches that gain favor in small Silicon Valley start-ups are quickly crushed in the Fortune 500. Since the computer is precise and unforgiving, the hacker can be too precise and equally unforgiving of human shortcomings. Yet in modern matrix organizations, it is people, not machines, that the hacker ultimately requires to accomplish the business task.

Apple Computer's manager of hardware development, Steve Sakoman, reaffirms the need for balanced technical people. Apple, the name most associated with the personal computer revolution, has a product development process that involves an intense team-based approach. "You need people who are technically excellent but broad enough to understand what others have to say, share goals, and exercise good people skills," says Sakoman. "Nerds need not apply. We don't look for the stereotypical engineer who sits off in a corner, never goes home, and sleeps on a mat."[12]

Ironically, hackers are not the best programmers. Most of today's programming actually involves designing tools for end users—in other words, those line business managers and clerical staffers whose technical expertise is shallow. Former college hackers ultimately find themselves understanding that to design business tools that are user friendly, the engineer must be user friendly.

Harrison proposes the following three rules for software organizations that would help bring hackers back into the fold as business people:

1. Everyone must be treated—and must behave—like a professional.
2. Everyone must be committed to the [business] objective.
3. Common sense must prevail.[13]

Another solution to this problem could of course be to train highly specialized computer programmers and engineers in various human relations and managerial skills. For some, this is a viable alternative over the long run.

It certainly cannot be seen as a quick fix. Because most companies want someone with more than just a slight taste for what business systems analysis involves, managers should also consider the personality characteristics and breadth of experience of candidates for technical positions during the hiring process. Seek someone who is literate and who can interact with other people. More education and broader team-based extracurricular and community activities tend to really make a difference here.

It is usually easier to train generalists in a specific skill than to train specialists to become broad-based, creative thinkers. We have no proof of this assertion other than many year's experience with people in the computer industry. Consider the experience of one large Midwestern manufacturing company that actually shifted its recruiting goals for systems analyst positions from industrial engineers, MBAs, and dual degree math/liberal arts majors to computer science majors exclusively. At the time, the company was seeking to reduce the enormous training expenses needed to convert generalists into computer specialists. After three years, the firm switched back to recruiting trainable generalists instead of computer scientists.

The company found that what it thought it wanted—warm bodies to churn out computer code—actually caused a shortage of solid business managers. As the computer scientists grew in tenure with the company, they were not growing in breadth. Repeated attempts to broaden them failed. Far too many of the recruits reached a career ceiling after three years, and the company's MIS department suffered over the long run. The business problems that systems analysts are called on to identify and solve required much more than the skills of computer programming; they required the ability to bridge the gap between the "techies" and top executives, to interview line managers, to make mental linkages of business functions and their interactions, and to foresee problems, synthesize solutions, and sell technical solutions to skeptical managers. The company found it extremely tough to teach these subjective skills to analytical people, and so it now recruits multidisciplined generalists who have proven abilities to learn new things.

When it comes to technology assessment, many companies are looking for a fairly unique individual who has a solid technical background but one who internalizes the dynamics of the business. As the facilitator of change, this person must be a risk taker—someone who has a vision of the organization and the drive to make that vision a reality. The analytical skills of the best computer scientists and operations researchers plus the ability to conceptualize multiple disciplines into a coherent whole are required. The person should be able to operate within the organization with political finesse and know enough about technology's trends and market positioning to be a tough negotiator with computer and electronics vendors. Because this person would operate as a business partner with line managers, a leader of matrix teams, and a manager of structured projects, the apparent dichotomy of skills would seem to rule out the hacker. The balance of talents is almost a panacea, and executives are willing to seek a high-tech entrepreneur who can bring the vigor and responsiveness of the small Silicon Valley start-up company to the Fortune 500.

Gifford Pinchot describes this person as an *intrapreneur,* as "any of the dreamers who do."[14] "Those who take hands-on responsibility for creating innovation of any kind within an organization. The intrepreneur may be the creator or inventor but is always the dreamer who figures out how to turn an idea into profitable reality." This is a powerful challenge to the traditional role of corporate MIS departments and a "double dare" to software professionals to toss off the image of the hacker. The technology assessment consultant as the catalyst of change, the integrator of technologies with business goals, and the master organizational salesperson must function as an intrepreneur to be truly effective.

SELLING YOUR TECHNOLOGY STRATEGY

Because a new technology strategy is, by definition, a radical change from the organizational norms, special attention needs to be given to influencing the organization to accept your proposal. Of course each person has his or her own style that has proven successful over time. So I seek not to provide a short course in selling or negotiation. However, experience has taught us that proposals cannot be presented cold to key decision makers. People need to feel they are a part of the process.

Internal and external consultants are much more effective when they function as business partners, collaborators, and facilitators. In other words, we seek not to sell an idea; we seek to work with the organization to jointly coalesce the technology strategy. This forces the consultant to learn the client's business and have a stake in the firm's success. Likewise, the collaborative consulting approach helps the key decision makers feel ownership in the new technology strategy.

We have found that subtle background collaboration goes a long way in helping people "buy into" proposals. Rather than offering a single proposal, try breaking the proposal up into a series of "white papers" and informal technology seminars over a longer period of time. For example, a successful approach for SSI has been obtaining the support of internal client "champions" who help subtly sell our ideas while providing valuable feedback in areas we may have overlooked.

Managers are a bit suspect of external consultants. As mentioned in the introduction, overselling of hyped ideas and missed expectations give them a reasonable right to feel this way. However, an internal champion, clearly on the client's team, adds to our credibility and gives the organization a sense that true collaborative consulting produced the strategy.

Specifically, an effective method to enlist the support of internal champions starts with an understanding of the differences in the thinking styles of these internal supporters. This allows the consultant to approach champions based upon the way they like to learn new information. Research by Allen Harrison and Robert Bramson at InQ Educational Materials of Oakland, California, identified five major styles of thinking common in American corporations.[15] They are the Synthesist, Idealist, Pragmatist, Analyst, and Realist.

Although my colleagues and I do not claim to be specialists in this area, we have found the Harrison-Bramson approach of knowing managers' thinking styles useful in gaining their support. A simplification of these types includes the following characteristics.

The Synthesist is the restless, creative, people-curious, diverger. Typically seen as the artistic or scientific visionary, this person loves playing the devil's advocate, enjoys debating simply for the intellectual exercise, and draws inferences from data to distill the essence of the issue. Seen by more "rational" people as having "off-the-wall" ideas, Synthesists occasionally exhibit brilliant flashes of insight.

Idealists are wholistic thinkers. They tend to see the big picture, are intuitive, receptive to new ideas, and are good consensus builders among divergent views. Their extremely high standards sometimes cause them to seek an ideal solution instead of the best one available. Idealists also have a heightened sense of the long-term view. Research indicates that many educators are found to have this thinking style.

The Pragmatist's approach to thinking may be found among some of the most prominent CEOs. A tendency toward immediate action, quick solutions, adaptation to new situations, and focusing on immediate payoffs are typical characteristics. The Pragmatist is interested in solving a problem by whatever means necessary. Elegant theories have use only when they can be tied to a real world solution, today.

The Analyst avoids risk and believes there is one and only one solution. This solution may be determined only by hard data. Facts are valued over feelings. Models, formulas, logic, and methods are important credibility builders. Analysts are detail oriented and tend to take a long time to come to a decision because they need more data. "Just one more study, benchmark, or test" is their approach to becoming comfortable with a new technology.

The empirical worldview—that only what can be seen, touched, heard, or smelled is real—is the hallmark of the Realist. Anything other than their own experience (or that of a credible witness) is fanciful. They don't want to hear about future releases of products, they want to see a demo now. Direct, forceful, a preference for activity over analysis, and a constant eye on objectives, costs, and benefits are typical of Realists.

With so many different views of the world, it should come as no surprise that most of the people you meet in a client's organization don't initially buy into your approach. For example, if a consultant is an Idealist presenting to a group of Analysts, probably too little data is included for their tastes. Action-oriented proposals are demanded by Pragmatists and Realists but carry little weight with Synthesists. Theory and vision may be needed to convince the Synthesist, but they will be devalued by the Pragmatist. A compromise approach that doesn't take into account the long-range view or the impact on the human element will be flatly rejected by the Idealist.

Since approximately 36 percent of the American population exhibits Idealist or Analyst thinking styles, 24 percent Realists, 18 percent Pragmatists, and only 11 percent Synthesists, it is wise for the consultant to remember that most people will not see a proposal in the same way and may be difficult to convince unless an approach unique to their style is taken.[16] In fact, many people exhibit more than one style. Since any meeting may have any or all of the styles in the room, total agreement is unlikely with a cold presentation.

SSI subscribes to the value inherent in these different thinking styles proposed by Harrison and Bramson. Instead of presenting our recommendations to the total group, we meet individually with decision makers and break up proposals into pieces that take advantage of the various styles of our internal champions. This ensures that when a presentation is given to the entire committee, each decision maker and key influencer has his or her personal information needs met. With this approach, people fully understand our proposals, and we are one step closer to project approval.

With a new technology that is untested in the organization or for a combination of technologies that seems revolutionary in its application, consider brainstorming the vision with an internal Synthesist. While working with a large marketing company, for example, I was asked to take on a risky project that integrated seven technologies into a total information management solution. Today's industry buzzword for the combination of technologies is *expert database systems*. Without getting into the proprietary details, let us say that it took advantage of internal numerical data, electronic mail, word processing, external videotex, graphics, database retrieval systems, and natural language queries.

Most of the firm's systems designers would not touch it with a stick. It was too speculative, did not have direct benefits to current projects, and was not supported by the organizational power brokers. However, we bounced the idea off the resident Synthesist, an ex-MIT professor whose job it was to think great thoughts. He loved it. It was just the type of challenge he enjoyed—wild, blue sky, intangible, with no immediate payoff. His enthusiasm spread to a network of these Synthesists inside the company, and they began introducing us to some of the best academic and industry researchers in each of the seven technology areas. For weeks, we traveled from coast to coast to the great think tanks of America discussing the possibilities. Internally, the champion was infecting people with a new enthusiasm. He was talking about a vision of the future with the key decision makers, and he was paving the way for a ground swell of credibility and demand for the technology by line managers. As a respected Synthesist, he helped us create a receptive environment for the new ideas.

The key learning is this—Synthesists are good allies for soft selling a new technology. Show them literature, give them demonstrations, speculate in lengthy brainstorming sessions with them, and visualize a new organization. You will be amazed at how primed your audience will be.

Another case involved a new data communications product for a Silicon Valley electronics company. My client's organization had responsibility for making engineering workstations communicate with IBM mainframes. Most of the software is a de facto standard with little room for creativity. So the task was not glamorous to the design engineers. The challenge for product managers was to match the actual customer needs to the myriad of features that could be implemented by the development engineers (who would just love to implement all of them to add some spice to their support work). The firm's customers had already told us what they wanted built; the challenge was to convince the organization of the urgency of the project. Where the traditional approach would have been to study the situation and develop a comprehensive product plan, a better approach was needed to sell what, at this point, was an unpopular but inevitable idea.

We published the results of our investigation in segments as preliminary drafts to the key influencers in the organization. These people were middle managers and senior technical people who would make or break a project by their recommendation to the division manager. A white paper on the customer needs was published and sent to the line managers responsible for profit, most of whom seemed to be Pragmatists, Realists, and/or Idealists. Another part of the proposal highlighting a new technology and a different approach to solving the customer need was put in non-threatening white paper form and sent to the marketing manager who seemed to be a Synthesist. The lab manager responsible for developing the solution was very skeptical and seemed like a Pragmatist, so we set up a series of meetings with customers so he could see the demand for himself. The action-oriented support manager was pleased to have an implementation plan that involved a great deal of third-party participation with detailed time lines, milestones, and contingency plans. The sponsoring manager, a cross between an Idealist and an Analyst, was very supportive after getting a report that covered all bases as a whole with detailed justification data and plans.

When the final report was issued and the presentation made to division management, little resistance surfaced to what was an unpopular idea. We are convinced that this method worked because the decision makers all had their needs for buy-in met in the way that best suited their approach to learning new information.

As a result of these learning experiences, it is clear to us that even the best technical idea will have limited acceptance unless people are supportive because of a collaborative effort at developing the idea. Harrison and Bramson's thinking styles are only one technique of many that help put a framework around technology transfer and selling new ideas in the organization. Each technology assessor will have to adapt this and other theories to his or her own successful styles and approaches. However, this should serve as further evidence that a technology strategy requires more than technology. The human element cannot be ignored.

KEEPING ABREAST OF CHANGING TECHNOLOGIES

Technology assessors must be able to learn new technologies as a daily matter of standard professional practice. Since technology is being developed at a fierce pace, it is clear that staying abreast of innovation will become a more difficult challenge. Indeed, we at SSI have found that the traditional educational approach that most of us learned in school desperately needs modification.

The education of technology assessors needs to be a lifelong process. Since American industry is beginning to accept the notion of increasing, often exponential change, twelve to nineteen years of school will not, in itself, prepare analysts, engineers, and managers to combat the threat of technical obsolescence.

Consider the 1982 finding by MIT researchers that in the fast-moving fields of computer science and electrical engineering, former whizzes, now middle-aged, find themselves fighting a losing battle to keep from falling behind intellectually. Engineers as young as thirty-five are increasingly expressing this concern. Each year some 10,000 or 5 percent of the nation's electrical engineers transfer out of their field.[17] Many leave because they feel useless and obsolete. Yet America is facing a shortage of more than 100,000 engineers. The gap is not likely to be closed simply by increasing the output of engineering schools, which are currently at their limit. A more reasonable alternative is to increase the productivity and retention of engineers already in the profession.

The MIT committee, chaired by Professor Robert Fano, recommended a quantum leap amounting to a revolution in engineering education. The committee proposed new alliances between businesses and engineering schools under which, on company time, engineers could continue their graduate-level education in at least one 15-week course per year. Universities were asked to adopt more flexible residency requirements so that at least 10 percent of engineers' working time could be devoted to continuing education, potentially at the workplace.[18]

American industry has heeded the spirit, if not the letter, of the MIT proposal. Most high-technology firms such as Bell Labs, General Electric, Wang, Digital, and Hewlett-Packard (HP) have joint education projects with universities. HP and Stanford University in Palo Alto, California, have an innovative arrangement whereby engineers may pursue doctoral degrees with company support. Universities, such as Northeastern in Boston, have opened extension programs in Silicon Valley that attract engineers and technicians from a wide range of smaller companies to their evening programs. Large electronics companies like DEC and IBM have substantial in-house training organizations that keep their people technically current, and the Wang Institute in Tyngsboro, Massachusetts, offers advanced degree programs.[19]

It comes as no surprise that high-tech companies understand the need to keep their best resources technically competent. For these companies, which produce new generations of products every eighteen months to three years, it is a matter of pure survival. Unfortunately, traditional industries like manufacturing, distribution, consumer marketing, and finance have been historically slower to embrace advanced education for its staff. This too is changing. Company-sponsored managerial and technical seminars, leaves of absence, short courses, co-op learning programs, and reimbursement of employees for evening degree programs are becoming common. As traditional industries realize that their competitiveness is becoming more dependent on the application of advanced technologies in manufacturing and on more creative use of information, we can expect to see a surge in career-long retraining.

Lifelong learning, therefore, is being accepted as necessary. At the same time, business leaders are growing concerned that the educational system has failed to teach the skills needed in today's radically changed high-tech world. The debate rages as to whether schools and universities should teach skills that will be marketable in industry or whether the primary purpose of education should be to produce liberally trained thinkers and generalists who can adapt to many industries or entrepreneurial endeavors. This latter charter would leave the business and technical training to industry. There is a hybrid school of thought that advocates a blend of both liberal arts and technical training.

Regardless of which argument one subscribes to, business and academic leaders need to face the reality of the need for a new approach to learning. The approach we advocate is rooted in an understanding that technological revolutions define different parameters and needs. The information society that faces America does not toss off the established educational system—indeed, it requires it to supply technically and socially literate citizens. But technology demands a restructuring of our approach to education to meet the needs and constraints of a new age. Half-hearted attempts at back-to-basics alone or vocational education alone will not begin to solve the problem. Instead, these attempts are likely to exacerbate them.

Managers must understand that the educational system in America was developed over hundreds of years to meet the needs of a rapidly industrializing economy. It taught millions of children how to obey instructions from an authority figure, how to be prompt, and how to adapt to rote, repetitive work. This is what futurist Alvin Toffler calls the "Covert Curriculum."[20] Although we were told that the curriculum was made up of the "three Rs"—reading, writing, and 'rithmetic—plus a dash of history, science, and possibly an introduction to a foreign language, the purpose of secondary (and some college) education was to prepare us for work in the mechanistic industrial world. Toward this end, our school system has served us well.

Today's rapidly changing information-intensive business environment, however, demands a new set of skills. Such skills include the highly analytical mathematical and scientific approaches plus the more creative visioning and intuitive skills that are difficult for an industrialized school system to teach. The most important skill is *learning how to learn* and then applying that learning to anticipatory visioning exercises.

An approach to learning new technologies that has worked for us at Strategic Systems involves supplementing traditional linear learning with a systematic educational process modified from one proposed by Joel de Rosnay in his work, *Le Macroscope*.[21] Using this approach with a multidisciplinary team can be an effective means of analysis. Consider the following seven points.

1. Avoid Exclusively Linear Learning Approaches

Traditional linear learning is based on the assumption that the way to understand the whole picture is to subdivide it into its smallest parts in the manner of the Cartesian approach advocated by René Descartes. On the contrary, we have found in our practice that a better way to approach a new technology is to review the material as a whole to get the total picture and then analyze each component. It is only when the work under study has been examined in total that we see the picture of a jigsaw puzzle and can appreciate its discrete parts.

The Cartesian assumption that the whole can be extrapolated from its parts has led to phenomenal successes in the physical sciences. "Yet, at the same time, all aspects of the human experience that did not fit into a predictable mechanical picture were set aside as non-empirical, non-scientific, or just not fit for scientific study," as the University of Minnesota's Michele Small notes.[22] This overemphasis on analysis can lead to a lack of awareness of wider human issues—issues that cannot be ignored especially when humans are expected to benefit from a new technology's application.

Concentration on smaller components, first, is one reason why too many people get bogged down in technology or outright fear it. To borrow an old cliché, they actually can't see the forest for the trees. As a result, many technical solutions get implemented that suboptimize a portion of the problem but either have no effect or have a detrimental effect on the total organization.

For example, a large high-tech manufacturing company implemented an automated flight reservation system that optimized the cost of business travel for its engineers and managers. A typical flight might have saved the company $100 or $200, but the firm's most expensive resource, its people, suffered in-flight routing delays, missed connections, and were forced to pay extra fares out of their own pockets when business travel needed to be changed with little notice. The system's optimization of airline fares caused it to seek out tickets that could not be changed within three days of the flight. The dynamics of the high-tech industry frequently cause schedule changes at the last minute. When this happened, staff were left to fend for themselves at remote airports.

As a result, four-hour flights were extended to twelve hours with two to three layovers and/or in-flight changes. Managers sometimes missed meetings. Engineers were forced to take "red-eye" flights that saved a couple hundred dollars but put them in no condition to effectively contribute to meetings the next day. In many cases, the staff had to pay extra fares en route to make scheduled meetings, so the company actually paid more for travel overall.

The bottom line is this: The system suboptimized one tangible aspect of the firm's business—airline fares—by trading off the effectiveness of its personnel. Although the financial manager who implemented the system was a hero to his organization, this could hardly be considered a technological benefit to the travelers.

2. Definitional Independence

Avoid definitions that are so precise that they limit the play of imaginations or polarize people. As previously discussed, precise definitions are crucial to the proper workings of science. Although critical to transferring scientific information, when applied to the real world of organizations and their application of new technology, rigid definitions force the mind into constraints. Such constraints force a mechanical set of assumptions that limits a technology's applicability.

Consider how Digital Equipment's *All-IN-1* product is commonly considered as an office automation tool. The system has many of the features that office workers have found valuable: word processing, electronic mail, filing, and an electronic calendar. But many analysts overlook the prime benefit of such office integration tools. This product embodies many of the features of a fourth generation "data highway." The *All-IN-1* system transparently converts information from databases and documents into a common format and makes it available to non-sophisticated users. By broadening the definition of the system, several companies have been able to find new applicability for what was incorrectly seen as "just another office system."

At least in the initial learning phases, removing restricting definitions allows many companies to view "progress" as more than "bigger and better" and to see that winning does not always mean that someone else must lose. It opens up a dialogue among people with different perspectives about what technology is and how it can be used. Sure, it may take more time to try alternatives and reach a consensus, but definitional independence also keeps us from overlooking a unique application with a high rate of return.

3. Analogous Systems

Stress the concepts of limits, interdependence, and mutual causality of events. Complicated systems may often be studied by drawing analogies with common systems. For example, communication networks may be seen as transportation highways or as the complex of veins and arteries that makes up the human body. Taking a systems perspective of common networks allows technology assessors to consider real-world examples of traffic jams, flow rates, and peak periods of use. Real-world analogies taken from integrated disciplines, such as biology, transportation, and economics, allow people to grasp networks that are more difficult to see (e.g., the flow of electrons). Using our everyday experiences as a base, it is much easier to understand and predict the behavior of complicated system components that are inherently related.

4. Thematic Integration

New technologies don't exist in isolation. It sometimes helps to integrate several technologies around a central core objective or theme. Such integration can produce unexpected insights or synergistic results by allowing the team to see applications that were not earlier perceived.

A major manufacturing and distribution company combined its electronic mail system, office workstations, corporate databases, public news wires, stock market data sources, and optical disk storage systems into a proprietary information center. By adding artificial intelligence systems that learned about the jobs and information requirements of managers, this unique information system provided much richer, more timely, and more accurate information that fit each manager's need and approach to his or her job. The firm never considered such a combination of technologies until it adopted a goal of giving "everyone the information needed, when and where they need it." With the theme of "direct information empowerment," the company's systems analysts were challenged to broaden their scope beyond the products that existed on the market, and, as a result, text, numerical data, graphics, and images were blended into a coherent information asset.

5. Facts Are Only Partial Indicators

This can be an especially tough point for managers with Pragmatic/ Analytic learning styles or those trained as engineers, accountants, or lawyers. Contrary to common assumptions, facts alone don't tell the whole story. An absolute requirement is a solid understanding of the relationships that link facts. A simple exercise noting who, what, when, where, why, and how the existing systems and organizational structures will be affected will help identify the relationships between a technology and its users. Knowing who or what will be affected sets the foundation for anticipation of who or what will benefit or suffer from a technological change and for a determination of the degree of the impact.

6. Objectivity Is a Myth

The technology assessor must realize that no observer is totally objective. Decisions may look as if they are made on the basis of analysis, but with a closer look, it becomes obvious that objectivity is a lofty goal that is seldom realized. A technology and a solution must be evaluated based on a clear understanding that hidden agendas and cultural, professional, political,and personal perspectives must be considered. Even for the so-called objective consultant, the act of observing changes the observed, and our interpretations of what we see are colored by our experiences. The best way to be objective is to recognize one's subjectivity and always take it into account in any analysis or decision.[23]

7. Intuition Is Valid

Allow for and encourage an intuitive, creative, non-rational approach to envisioning alternative technology applications.

Our examination of the major scientific paradigms of the past 500 years has shown a growth and expansion in thought from the Aristotelian to the Newtonian and now the holistic paradigms. We have seen that our new worldview demands the use of our entire brain, not just the left or right hemisphere. Synthesis of thought is crucial for modern survival. As culture grows more complex, science all-encompassing, and choices more diverse, we need whole-brain understanding as we never needed it before. We need the right brain to innovate, sense, dream, and envision; and the left to test, analyze, check out, and build constructs and supports for the new order of thinking. "Together they invent the future," Marilyn Ferguson asserts.[24]

New paradigms arise through the checks and balances inherent in the structure of the scientific method and its community's inner workings. However, such shifts in belief are closely associated with a creative minority within the community, some of whom may have formulated their ideas as a result of insight. Just as Descartes and Newton are said to have put all the fragments of physical and mathematical data together to form their individual theories, today's scientist is occasionally the benefactor of insight or intuition.

Either as a result of severe inconsistencies in experimental results or as a result of stress at a time of deep contemplation of the nature of scientific problems, modern technology assessors use their creative right brains to synthesize data into new perspectives of old phenomena.

In most of our lives, insight has been accidental. We wait for it as our forebears awaited lightning to make fires. But making mental connections is our most crucial learning tool. The essence of human intelligence is to forge links, go beyond the given, see patterns, relationships, and context. The natural consequences of these subtle workings of the mind is insight.[25]

THE ONGOING CHANGE PROCESS

Technology assessors must view organizational change as a natural response to dynamic competitive pressures. However, this worldview must be accompanied by an expectation that there will be resistance to change by the client organization.

Many people feel that the introduction of new technology will have a negative impact on the workplace. Some managers resist technical change because they view it as adding an element of uncertainty and risk to proven methods that have served them well over the years. Resistance also forewarns of areas that need more or less attention. Others fear that technology will depersonalize the workplace and threaten their jobs.

It is true that, if poorly planned and implemented, technology can cause (and has caused) unnecessary dislocations, inefficiency, and low employee morale. But when organizations implement technology properly, risk can be reduced by adding a new dimension of flexibility that was previously unavailable to the firm. Effective implementation of new technology can help manufacturing departments work more closely with product designers, provide information to a broad range of individuals at various levels in the organizational chain so they may perform tasks more effectively, and reduce the drudgery of routine work by automation.

The key to successful technology implementation goes beyond mere hardware devices and software applications. In fact, a corporate culture of innovation with adequate inclusion of the affected parties—managers, users, and support personnel—in decision making should be weighed in the technology assessment process on par with the technologies. By innovation we mean the generation, implementation, and acceptance of new ideas, processes, products, and services as a normal part of doing business in a changing world. It involves the commercial application of previous scientific knowledge, existing inventive work, and experimental development for financial gain. Participation by the affected parties (those who will use, manage, and maintain the proposed system) has been shown by William Kraus and Nicholas Weiler to be an effective deterrent to resistance.[26]

In a company with an innovative culture, change is seen as an accepted part of doing business. Indeed, change represents opportunity and a chance to seize the moment, introduce a new product, expand markets, and thwart competitors' encroachments. Without change, the firm cannot grow, career options are limited, and people stagnate.

Innovative companies structure themselves like self-correcting organisms. They have the flexibility to respond to change, and their people have the freedom to act without requesting approval from a corporate committee. Firms that are change oriented will have a large number of mechanisms that encourage the fluidity of organizational boundaries. Ideas flow freely. Not all change is triggered by problems; people with ideas, techniques, and technologies are encouraged to go out and seek new opportunities to move the business ahead. Such organizations are receptive to the change-facilitator role that technology assessors play.

Their counterparts are the change-resisters. In such companies, what has worked before is expected to continue to work into an indefinite future. The basic assumptions and the structure of decisions seek to protect the organization against unnecessary change. Rosabeth Moss Kanter notes that this style, this mode of organizing, ensures that change-resisters will repeat what they already know. For activities that should be repeated—the areas of high certainty of routine—habitual action is efficient and desirable. But the business environment is constantly changing, and the growth and dispersion of technology accelerates the competitive pressures in many industries. So the static culture of the change-resisters makes it extremely difficult to move beyond its existing capacity and self-imposed constraints in order to improve and innovate. In Kanter's words, such cultures "inhibit the entrepreneurial spirit and makes the organization a slave of its past."[27]

Companies that resist change pose a serious problem for technology assessors. If the technology implementation effort is to have any chance of success and provide visible benefits to the organization, the technology assessor must first help static firms value change. The technology assessor, whether external consultant or internal systems analyst, must draw upon interpersonal, collaborative, negotiative, and selling skills. These skills must be focused to help the firm view departures from tradition as an additional brick in the foundation of experience that positions the company to deal with new problems as they arise. In addition, the firm is building experience that will allow its people to replace existing processes with more productive ones. Unless this recognition exists and is viewed as desirable, it makes no sense to start down a path of eventual project failure.

Another strong argument for accepting change is rooted in the current upheaval that American companies face. Even the most conservative of firms will admit that the rules of international business today force every enterprise to do some deep introspection about the nature of its competition. In the future, the products made in advanced nations will derive less of their value from either blue-collar labor or capital goods. "More product value will come from the quality of thought and innovation that go into them," according to Gifford Pinchot, author of *Intrapreneuring*.[28] As we have already seen with electronics, steel, and textiles, the more often information on how to make existing products is dispersed, old and unchanging industries will continue to migrate from industrially advanced nations to less developed ones. American industry will not be able to effectively compete on a basis of cheap labor and abundant raw materials. So, according to Pinchot, American industry will have to compete based on how well we can do things differently. Like it or not, we are on an innovation "treadmill," notes Pinchot.

Once it is accepted that change is an inescapable reality, what can be done to overcome the organizational barriers to new technologies? Kraus and Weiler of General Electric give suggestions in six key areas. They found in a 1985 study of seventy organizations in the United States and Japan that technical knowledge and expertise are not the key factors in successful technology implementations. Managing the human and organizational barriers in the following areas are crucial:

1. *Business Need/Opportunity Definition.* Support is gained by having the problem defined at the highest possible level in the organization. However, when the end user of the system defines the problem, the solution has a better chance of success. So technology assessors can maximize the probability of success by defining the solution in a way that meets the need of both groups.

2. *Organizational Environment.* Always define the success of the project in terms of specific goals that are valuable to the user. Technologies implemented without a clear concern for the user's business are seen as an attempt to advance the technology for its own sake, and it is justifiably resisted.

3. *Implementation Team.* The team approach greatly enhances implementation and promotes a feeling of user "buy-in."

4. *Installation Plan.* Follow a realistic plan. It should build on past suc-

cesses, progress at a rate the organization can absorb, anticipate and manage obstacles, and include user-education processes.

5. *End-User Ownership.* Involving users early in the system's implementation reduces the risk for the users, builds a feeling of ownership and collaboration, and helps the implementors to tailor training to the end-users' specific needs and learning styles. It also prepares the end users for acceptance of long-term operational responsibility.

6. *Vendor Integration.* Resistance can be reduced by enlisting vendors that can offer products tailored to the organization's unique needs rather than asking the users to adapt to an off-the-shelf solution.[29]

Technology resistance is something to be expected. It is often a legitimate forum for highlighting real organizational problems that must be corrected. Kraus and Weiler remind us that resistance frequently "stems from knowledgeable perception of items that have been overlooked" but must be addressed.[30] When technology assessors function less as technocratic hackers and more like technically astute intrapreneurs, they will learn to anticipate human and organizational resistance. With the "people issues" addressed, new technologies can be successfully planned and managed for increased client competitiveness.

NOTES

1. "Management Discovers the Human Side of Automation," *Business Week* (September 29, 1986), p. 72.

2. Rosabeth Moss Kanter, *The Change Masters: Innovation and Entrepreneurship in the American Corporation* (New York: Simon & Schuster, 1983), pp. 17-36.

3. Ibid., p. 18.

4. Ibid., p. 19.

5. Sherry Turkle, *The Second Self: Computers and the Human Spirit* (New York: Simon & Schuster, 1984), pp. 196-238.

6. Ibid., pp. 213-14.

7. William Harrison, "Over the Rainbow in a Software Garage Shop," *Computerworld* (1986).

8. Margie E. Wells-Davis, personal interview with author, October 1987, San Francisco.

9. Everett M. Rogers and Judith K. Larsen, *Silicon Valley Fever: Growth of High-Technology Culture* (New York: Basic Books, 1984), pp. 137-276.

10. Ibid., p. 165.

11. Ibid., p. 154.

12. Bro Uttal, "Speeding New Ideas to Market," *Fortune* (March 2, 1987), p. 66.

13. Harrison, "Over the Rainbow in a Software Garage Shop."

14. Gifford Pinchot III, *Intrapreneuring: Why You Don't Have to Leave the Corporation to Become an Entrepreneur* (New York: Harper & Row, 1985).

15. Allen Harrison, and Robert M. Bramson, *Styles of Thinking* (New York: Doubleday Book Company, 1981).

16. Ibid.

17. "Are Whizzes Washed Up at 35?" *Time* (October 18, 1982), p. 100.

18. Robert M. Fano, James D. Bruce, William M. Siebert, and Louis D. Smullin, *Lifelong Cooperative Education: Report of the Centennial Study Committee* (Cambridge, Mass.: The MIT Press, 1982).

19. An Wang, *Lessons: An Autobiography* (Reading, Mass.: Addison-Wesley, 1986), p. 235.

20. Alvin Toffler, *The Third Wave* (New York: William Morrow, 1980), pp. 22-248.

21. Joel de Rosnay, *Le Macroscope: Vers une vision globale* [*The Macroscope: Towards a Global Vision*] (Paris: Editions du Seuil, 1975).

22. Michele G. Small, "Toward a Systematic Education," *Through the 80s* (Washington, D.C.: The World Future Society, 1980), p. 344.

23. Ibid., p. 349.

24. Marilyn Ferguson, *The Aquarian Conspiracy* (Los Angeles: J.P. Tarcher, 1980), pp. 145-300.

25. Ibid.

26. William A. Kraus and Nicholas W. Weiler, "Overcoming Human and Organizational Barriers to New Technology," *Tappi Journal* (Vol. 68, No. 12, December 1985), pp. 26-29.

27. Kanter, *The Change Masters*, p. 31.

28. Pinchot, *Intrapreneuring*, p. 8.

29. Kraus and Weiler, "Overcoming Human and Organizational Barriers to New Technology," pp. 26-27.

30. Ibid., p. 29.

6

Key Technologies and the Company of the Future

THE FUTURE CORPORATE ENVIRONMENT

The corporation of the future is likely to experience an accelerated rate of change. Competition will be increasingly global in scope. Costs will need to be cut; non-productive plants and processes overhauled; and better ways must be found to produce the goods and services that customers demand. Targeting product and service offerings to finer market segments will require more and better information in a timely fashion. Organizations will become flatter (i.e., less hierarchical) and leaner.

Business functions that were once valued for their unique skill sets will become more routine. Such routine work will be increasingly automated so that more work can be done with fewer people. This trend has always existed in industry, but new technologies will place structure around formerly unstructured subjective problems, forcing people and companies to compete on new bases. Although business units will be smaller and more flexible, we expect to see a renewed emphasis on the value of human creativity.

We have also shown that technical innovation can be used to support human decision-making processes and value chain activities. Technology can be both an augmenter of existing business functions and a lever, opening the gates to new, unforeseen markets and opportunities. Surpassing mere automation, technology will often drive future business opportunities. As a result, executives are likely to increase the role of technologists in strategy formulation.

As American industry faces the growing challenge to its traditional leadership, there will be an increased need to concentrate less on cost-based competition and more on the competitive advantage provided by creatively applying technologies to common applications. Foreign competitors will wage a constant struggle to produce products with more features, of higher quality, and at a lower cost. As we have seen with the legion of industries that have moved offshore, America can no longer compete on economies of scale alone; it must compete based on the quality of the thought process that goes into producing products and on tailoring service offerings to the specialized needs of individual customers. This will require appropriate attention to business trends, human values, and technical developments.

MIS organizations are in a unique position to step to the forefront and offer sorely needed technical leadership, but what about the creativity required to balance technical, organizational, and business issues? The technical infrastructure is in place. Corporate MIS has spent the last three decades building an information repository, and, especially during the 1980s, these groups have teamed with telecommunications professionals to extend the span of data access and management control to even the most remote locations where business is conducted. Out of necessity, business decisions are being made at the lowest practical level in the organization, and friendlier (or at least normal-to-use) application programs and distributed computing power is providing the tools for what amounts to an organizational revolution. Computer and communications vendors have provided a constant stream of revolutionary equipment. New, powerful, small, and inexpensive hardware and innovative software are introduced, then used to their maximum benefit, mature, and are replaced by higher performing innovations in as little as eighteen months. The pace of technical development is staggering.

In spite of this accelerating pace, business leaders and users have managed to keep abreast of the latest technology. In the early 1980s, few line managers in a limited number of industries could be thought of as "technically literate." Using computers on a regular basis was the purview of specialists. Reactions from line managers and executives ranged from keyboard finger fumbling, to mistrust, to outright panic. Today, these same managers have become adept at computer usage and experienced at information selection and manipulation. They demand a voice in systems design and, in many cases, know as much about new developments and applications as systems specialists of the past. Many line managers have accepted the challenge of computer literacy and exceeded it. With such an infrastructure of data, networking, powerful computing platforms, normal-to-use application software, and technically astute end users, America has the basic building blocks in place for using information as, certainly, a corporate asset but quite possibly as a business weapon in an increasingly competitive international marketplace.

If industry rises to the challenge of international markets, it will become painfully clear that competition can no longer be waged on the cost advantages of massive capacity. Most American companies make products that other nations can easily match. According to Sven Arndt of the American Enterprise Institute, "U.S. producers tend to lose competitiveness, whether in textiles or electronics, when the technologies are established . . . when the product becomes a commodity. The United States remains competitive where the quality of the product depends on the human capital inputs."[1]

Therefore, U.S. industries need to stake their futures on products in which concerns about labor costs and foreign exchange rates are secondary to design, inventiveness, and customer value. To survive against increasingly stiff world competition requires that firms attract buyers through superior design and service, not through prices lower than those of the competition. Competitive advantage today and certainly in the future will come from the quality of the firm's products, services, and decisions. We are being challenged to work, not only harder, but also smarter. It is the creative use of information that allows people to work smarter.

Modern MIS organizations are facing up to the challenge of technology; now they must place the same emphasis on creativity. This has been an area of benign neglect by most systems organizations and discouragement by others. An environment that fosters innovation has been lacking. American business needs a culture of ongoing self-renewal where change is normal, expected, welcomed, and exploited.

Most managers insist that they encourage creative thinking among their systems professionals. But experts, such as Brandeis University professor Teresa Amabile, contend that the majority of managers squelch innovation at every turn.[2] Managers unknowingly raise eyebrows at ideas with any hint of impracticality. They have often made people feel constantly evaluated, restricted systems analysts from choosing their own approaches to problem solving, and fostered a sense of competition within groups at a time when teamwork is the key to innovation. Likewise, by isolating themselves in hacker havens, systems designers have often lacked the shared sense of mission of the organization and somehow missed the bigger picture of what the firm is trying to accomplish.

Successful firms will need to take advantage of the diversity inherent in the American workforce. An encouraging trend that we at SSI have noticed is more cross-pollination between the best technical minds of the MIS department and successful middle managers with profit-and-loss accountability. This gives technical people a better business focus and provides nontechnical managers with a broader view of what is technically possible and what is not. Teams are being formed with people with diverse thinking styles, consciously selected by management to use the creative tension inherent in their radically different views of the world to achieve a common goal. These groups are also linking up with customers to develop business solutions instead of merely computerized products. It is a welcome change from a tradition where computer vendors and MIS staffers developed products first, then looked for an applicable market. This matching of actual business needs to innovative technologies, creatively applied by matrix teams of people with diverse backgrounds and charters, is an example of working smarter.

Technology assessment provides a methodology to work smarter. By optimizing technology selection and integrating it with the demands of the business and the needs of the organization's people, the firm has a framework for capturing a distinct advantage over its competitors. Some of the most important technologies that could shape the nature of competitiveness over the next five years are (1) smaller, more powerful distributed computers; (2) transparent standardized computer communications networks; (3) better mass storage and retrieval of diverse information forms; and (4) artificial intelligence.

DEVELOPMENTS TO WATCH

Powerful Microprocessors

It is common to find computer-chip makers searching after an elusive goal of faster chips, smaller processors, and more powerful computers at lower prices. In fact, that has been the one constant factor that characterizes the industry. For example, SUN Microsystems offers a 10 MIP (millions of instructions per second) engineering workstation at a reasonable price, and Advanced Micro Devices announced a 32-bit chip that uses RISC (reduced instruction set) design to run at a sustained 17 MIPS.[3] The race goes on! Regardless of vendor, the S-Curve for microchips is short indeed, and indications are that new, higher performing technologies will force computer-chip technology to change to entirely new S-Curves in shorter time frames. Fortunately for the corporate consumer, we can depend on a steady stream of more powerful computers in smaller packages for the foreseeable future.

For instance, scientists at Bell Laboratories have implemented a VLSI (Very Large Scale Integration) computer chip with enough power to embed expert systemlike inferences not in software, as is common in the AI field, but on a single chip. According to its developers Masaki Togai and Hiroyuki Watanabe, the expert systems chip can perform 80,000 "fuzzy" inferences per second—approximate reasoning that allows it to cope with uncertainty.[4] Such hard-wired rule-based systems could allow for real-time computers to be miniaturized and placed in factory floor robots, for example.

Gallium arsenide (GaAs), a more radiation-hard and less temperature sensitive technology, offers the potential for computer chips about half an order of magnitude faster than the fastest silicon chip consuming the same power.[5] Josephson junction microchips, a technology that requires operation in extremely low temperatures, are now operable in an instrumentation workstation by Hypres, Inc.[6] The Hypres signal processor can capture and analyze electronic waveforms with picosecond cycle times. This could open up a world of precise communications and higher resolution video applications and could allow high-precision analog-to-digital conversion devices to improve quality testing processes.

Optics could further reduce the size and increase the power of computers by a thousandfold. Some of the research at the Lawrence Livermore weapons labs in California is focused on creating an optical device analogous to a transistor, according to William Broad in his book *Star Warriors*, which looks at the lives of the scientists at this secure facility.[7] Transistors turn electrical currents on and off. They are the building blocks of all silicon chips and therefore all computers. The power of computers comes from millions of transistors switching on and off at once; thus switching speed is one of the fundamental limits of computer speed. The best transistor switches in about a billionth of a second. Theoretically, an optical transistor could switch in a trillionth of a second and run on laser light. A computer built with these light-based transistors could solve a problem in a few minutes that would take days to solve on conventional computers. Such speculation is a bit far-fetched for the tastes of most commercial MIS staffers; however, because the Strategic Defense Initiative would benefit from such a device, it is likely to get enough funding to either prove or disprove the concept.[8]

If it is feasible, optical computers with the power of today's Cray super-computers could be made small enough to fit in the nose cone of a missile and, like most technologies, eventually find applications in industry. Pattern recognition could be improved for better online quality testing.[9] Optical associative memory could retrieve full information with only part of it being specified.[10] Robots with powerful microprocessors could operate in real time and sift through vast information bases stored in optical memory in fractions of a second, allowing for advanced artificial intelligence. The processing power provided by optical computers could allow more complex algorithms to be manipulated quickly for speech recognition. Humans could then speak to computers with various accents, inflections, and at different speeds.

The trend in computing is clearly toward entire special-purpose application systems on a single microchip. When this happens, computers will permeate common devices and industrial controls. This means that common household electronic devices will get smarter, and business systems will be able to handle more complex tasks. The knowledge of the world's top experts will be brought to your desk, and you will have the power to manipulate the accumulated knowledge of the Library of Congress. The power of today's supercomputers will fit neatly in a device half the size of a personal computer. This power will be seemingly limitless, yet there is likely to be demand for even more computing power for more vastly complicated applications.

Communications Networks

Computer communications networks have garnered a significant level of attention over the past two years. Computer users, executives, and the computer industry itself have finally recognized that organizational effectiveness depends on more than processing data. It requires human-to-human, human-to-organization, and human-to-system communications. Part of this recognition came about because of a realization that many of the desired information interactions were actually inhibited by the vehicle for transferring information—the organization's communications infrastructure.

The ability of computers to communicate instructions, share files, invoke application programs dispersed over the network, and tie the corporate information resources together rests squarely with its computer networking and telecommunications. Yet, because the computer and communications equipment vendors offered products that were unable (and many are still unable) to communicate with each other, customers found themselves with disjointed information islands. Unable to connect and share data, corporate computer users experienced severe information flow constraints. The screams were loud, and the vendors are now reacting to the cries.

International standards organizations, customer "cartels" such as the MAP (Manufacturing Automation Protocol) committee led by General Motors, and vendor cooperation is leading to common communications media, interfacing, and software. Computers from multiple vendors can now be connected and share information files. Many allow the users of one vendor's system to transparently access the applications on another vendor's system. The industry is at the connectivity phase and will be moving, albeit slowly, toward *interoperability*. In this latter state, any computer will be able to link up with another computer. They will surpass the data sharing and terminal emulation functionality of today to allow programs and processes to "attach" to each other and operate as a single application. Users will one day be able to request information without having to know where the information is located in the network, what format it is in, and what background manipulations and conversions the computers do to present it on the screen. They will also be able to access that information easily, without the need for technical specialists as intermediaries.

Computer, telephone, and cable TV/teleconferencing communications networks will continue to merge. Future communications media, such as fiber optics, lasers, satellites, and wires made from superconducting materials, will also enhance our abilities to quickly and inexpensively transfer larger volumes of information in various forms including text, numeric, voice, color graphics, images, and full-motion video over vast distances. For example, a research group at Nippon Telegraph and Telephone in Tokyo successfully transmitted data without amplification at 400 megabits per second over a single optical fiber nearly 300 kilometers long. Until then, the longest span had been just over 200 kilometers. Continued developments at this rate could allow future communications by thousands of users and computers at high speeds over a single fiber transferring documents, pictures, and video, in addition to voice conversations.[11]

Cable television and satellite communications will be used for more than just video transmission. For example, Project Stargate, the brainchild of Lauren Weinstein, a Los Angeles communications consultant, was designed to distribute Usenix Association's printed news via satellite.[12] Because it takes advantage of the unused portion of cable television's satellite uplink facility, Stargate demonstrates how a global distribution of not only network news but also corporate information is possible. Satellite facilities could be used to distribute software to all of a company's locations simultaneously, vastly simplifying centralized management of distributed computers. As satellite receivers get smaller and become integrated with other facilities, such as cellular communications, computers will become truly portable and still have access to, literally, a world of information.

Database Management and Optical Infobases

Database storage and management systems are among the most vital computer applications. Over the past two decades, data storage on magnetic disks has experienced capacity increases, improved reliability, and reduced access and retrieval times. Database management systems (DBMS) have allowed for faster direct access to information and provided the framework for ensuring data integrity and security. However, the amount of data stored is often insufficient for large complex uses, such as graphical database retrieval systems; and response times, like those found in context sensitive or full-text retrieval searches, can be slow.[13] In addition, today's databases clumsily manage compound information forms (text, numbers, images, voice, and the like) and poorly represent activities that vary with time.

A massive amount of information in various forms can be stored on optical disks at relatively low prices (inexpensive per byte of data compared with magnetic media). Bruce Berra and Nikos Troullinos of Syracuse University expect to see a 10-gigabyte (10 billion bytes) drive for about $10,000 in the near future.[14] This is a substantial savings over magnetic disk drives, whose densities are measured in megabytes (millions of bytes).

Optical disks, the descendants of popular audio compact disks, not only offer large storage densities, but the inherent speed and parallelism of light waves allow information to be carried at various wavelengths in the gigahertz range without interference. Access to data can be achieved quickly because the read/write head of a future optical drive could be deflected from track to track very rapidly, the non-interference of light would allow many beams to be carried on a single disk-drive head, and a non-focused beam could simultaneously read data from more than one point on the disk surface. Accessing data on an optical disk could be theoretically achieved in 100 microseconds, and data could be transferred as fast as 300 megabytes per second, according to Berra and Troullinos.[15]

Although the current commercial CD-ROM (compact disk, read-only-memory) technology is limited to reading data that has been written once—making it suitable for a limited range of archival, library, product catalog, educational, legal, and financial applications where information is unchanging and integrity is required—this new optical technology certainly has the ability to open up computer-based applications to a larger and richer set of information. As the technology develops, we can expect to see more reliable and cost-effective read/multiple-write capabilities. IBM and Matsushita are the current front-runners in the race for erasable optical disks.[16] With a richer information source, surpassing just text or numeric data to include other information forms such as images, we will move from applications of mere databases to the more generic concept of infobases. This technology includes integrated text, graphics, images (including handwritten signatures), and voice in digital form, capable of being manipulated by computer and directly accessible in a non-linear fashion for support of thinking patterns that are inherently non-linear.

In addition to new developments in information storage media, database management systems are expected to improve. For example, Richard Snodgrass of the University of North Carolina and Iisoo Ahn of Bell Laboratories speculate that future databases will have temporal capabilities.[17] Current databases supposedly model reality, but they lack the ability to record and process time-varying aspects of the real world. They are restricted to costly maintenance backups, checkpoints, and transaction logs to preserve past data states. The addition of a temporal capability could allow for improved historical queries, trend analysis,and embedding causal relationships among events.

Database access will be vastly improved by advanced application of new computing approaches such as parallel processing. A conventional computer executes algorithms and instructions serially. Because each step is executed one-at-a-time, computers have to be extremely fast and/or the database must be ordered in a manner that contributes to the efficiency of the database search process. Parallel processing would allow many computers to access data and work on parts of a problem simultaneously. All processors could execute the same algorithm concurrently, allowing for efficient access to disorganized data. For example, an Association for Computing Machinery report notes that a parallel processor with 65,536 processing elements called *The Connection Machine* by the Thinking Machines Corporation can perform a 20,000-term Boolean query against a 15-gigabyte freetext database in three minutes.[18]

Combining parallelism with sophisticated database indexing techniques can be expected to further increase the access speed of a typical parallel processor. By many computers working on the same problem at the same time, they should be able to solve it faster than a single computer working alone. This could vastly improve our abilities to apply numerical analysis, graphics, image processing, and artificial intelligence technologies to a broader range of problems.

Artificial Intelligence

Artificial intelligence will continue in importance and ultimately permeate business applications. Earlier chapters discussed how industry is horizontally integrating AI in a broad range of functional areas. Expert systems are being used to capture the knowledge of scarce human resource expertise. Such expertise can then be leveraged as computerized assistants in executive decision support, financial portfolio risk assessment, loan application analysis and real-time process control to standardize product quality in the chemical and food industries.

Natural languages and voice recognition systems are beginning to provide "normal" human interfaces to computers, and AI systems are helping to assist the decision-making processes by imposing structure on unstructured problems. We expect to see enhanced applications along these lines. But AI will also be integrated vertically and embedded in conventional computer technologies to drastically improve performance. Consider the following example of AI applications coming to prominence in the short term.

Information retrieval systems that search and present full-text news stories, journal articles, research reports, and financial statistics find information based on key words and index entries that correlate with the requestor's query. However, there is often a poor correspondence between the information that is needed and that presented by the system. Users typically receive too much irrelevant information or not enough of the right information. Advances in database indexing techniques can one day be augmented with artificial intelligence to provide the retrieval system with a better representation of the concepts implied by the user's request.

S.K.M. Wong and Wojciech Ziarko of the University of Regina speculate that database retrieval systems could, in fact, learn from their users and, over time, make judgments about the content of documents. This could allow automated retrieval systems to select documents without the requestor having to review them beforehand.[19] When linked with the corporate electronic mail system, an expert system could make judgments on the relevancy of retrieved information to various individuals based on current or related projects, research interests, departmental objectives, competitive analyses, or personal interests, and prioritize routing of the information to the appropriate people in the organization.

Artificial intelligence in the form of expert systems has an important place in telecommunications and computer networking. Keeping people communicating and information flowing is a vastly complicated task. A tremendous amount of knowledge is needed to design, operate, and troubleshoot networks. Telephone companies and other large organizations face the problems of operating unique, complex, heterogeneous networks with little or no overall control. Skilled people are required to design and manage these networks. Such experts are scarce and tend to change jobs frequently.[20] An expert system that captures their knowledge is quite attractive.

Because much of the needed information is available in electronic form, systematic network operation is feasible. Expert systems are being developed to ensure the sustained reliability of information flow. In addition, the ability to diagnose problems and raise the availability of communications lines may actually reduce the cost associated with redundancy in the network. Current applications include *Smart* from Bell Communications Research which allows network managers to monitor, analyze, and isolate network problems.[21] It also maintains a knowledge base of what to do about problems and off-loads problems from human consultants by intercepting and fielding questions from technicians. AT&T's *Nemesys* optimizes long-distance network performance during peak hours and advises operators which lines should be rerouted.[22] Digital Equipment's internal *Network Troubleshooting Consultant* can ask another program on a remote computer to diagnose itself.[23] Bolt Beranek and Newman offers an expert system called *Designet* that helps design communications networks.[24]

Artificial intelligence will continue to find favor in robotics. For example, one company developing AI products is focusing on robotic systems that can go into high-risk environments such as nuclear power plants. The *Surbot* by Remote Technology can perform visual, sound, temperature, and radiation-level readings while recording an inspection on videotape.[25]

Robotics will be integral to future factories. Sales of industrial robots are expected to grow from $500 million in 1986 to $5.8 billion in 1995.[26] In the future, we can expect artificial intelligence to be used to help robots become more flexible workers. They will be able to visually recognize objects, inspect them, and manipulate and assemble components with less explicit instructions from their programmers.

To sense, recognize, and plan manipulation strategies of objects, robots need to use data from multiple sensors in real time and knowledge of objects in the task environment. Currently, however, robot vision systems rely on models generated in an ad hoc manner with a limited scope. Only one representation of an object is used, thereby restricting a robot's ability to efficiently and reliably represent and recognize different classes of objects. Robot vision systems in operation today typically use models that cannot be easily applied to other objects or even objects of similar types with minor variations in their descriptions, according to Bir Bhanu of Honeywell.[27]

There is a potential solution to what is, in effect, a lack of integration of current technologies. This is a case where the fundamental building blocks are in place. Because robots operate in a fairly restricted domain where most objects are limited in number, predictable, and easily discernible, AI techniques are attractive. What is needed, however, is a better means to make judgments about objects regardless of their physical position on the manufacturing line and even when a portion of the object is hidden from view. Computer-aided design (CAD) models stored in the engineering database provide the raw 3D information needed. If linked to the computers that control factory robots, these engineering drawings would make an excellent starting point for robots to "learn" about objects they are likely to encounter. So the success of factory robots will depend in part on the integration of artificial intelligence for pattern recognition with computer vision, CAD models, sensors, and mechanical manipulator technologies.

CONCLUSION

As noted throughout this book, technology assessment need not be viewed as some mystical art or a precise science. Considering it as technically astute, commonsense strategic management is a more pragmatic approach and a more accurate description.

In essence, technology assessment can best be summarized in this manner: Technology assessors, whether external consultants or internal MIS analysts, need to spend time at the end-user location getting to know the business and the people. Needs and opportunities, problems, and promising strengths should be noted. Focus on the firm's vision, its goals, and the components of client processes and products that add value to the client's customers. Simultaneously, technology assessors need to immerse themselves in technologies that could affect the client. Visit experts, attend conferences, carry out secondary research, and build prototype systems. Be experienced in learning how to learn; then no technology should be beyond the consultant's grasp (at least at the conceptual level). Make use of information retrieval technology and prototypes to match technical developments with business opportunities. Recommendations need to be reviewed by a multidisciplinary team for a broader perspective (we call it a "sanity check"). Insist on including a study of how people in the organization are likely to react to the new technology and changes in established procedures. One cannot overlook an examination of what the client's competitors are doing with technology and what restrictions are established by government agencies. By all means, throughout each phase keep clients and decision makers informed as partners in the process. These are the commonsense steps in any technology assessment process.

It is clear in today's highly competitive marketplace that change will occur! So the only decision left to managers who want their organizations to remain healthy is not whether but HOW they will use technology to exploit the inevitable opportunities made available by change. It is Strategic Systems' goal to make our clients winners *in business* via technology utilization, not technology havens per se. We have found that being aware of the issues and considerations raised in this book, following a rational technology assessment process with a multiskilled team, and by asking the right questions of the right people, we can turn lackluster strugglers into competitive champions.

NOTES

1. Oswald Johnston, "Superior Products May Be U.S. Trade Deficit Solution," *Los Angeles Times* (September 22, 1986).

2. David H. Freedman, "Cultivating IS Creativity," *Infosystems* (July 1987), pp. 24-25.

3. Alexander Wolfe and Bernard C. Cole, "World's Fastest Microprocessor," *Electronics* (March 19, 1987), p. 61.

4. Masaki Togai and Hiroyuki Watanabe, "Expert System on a Chip: An Engine for Real-Time Approximate Reasoning," *IEEE Expert* (Institute of Electrical and Electronic Engineers, Fall 1986), pp. 55-62.

5. Veljko Milutinovic, "GaAs Microprocessor Technology," *Computer* (Institute of Electrical and Electronic Engineers, October 1986), pp. 10-11.

6. Samuel Weber, "Found! A Practical Way to Turn Out Josephson Junction Chips," *Electronics* (February 19, 1987), pp. 49-53.

7. William J. Broad, *Star Warriors: A Penetrating Look into the Lives of the Young Scientists Behind Our Space Age Weaponry* (New York: Simon & Schuster, 1985), p. 64.

8. Ibid.

9. Trudy E. Bell, "Optical Computing: A Field in Flux," *IEEE Spectrum* (Institute of Electrical and Electronic Engineers, August 1986), pp. 34-57.

10. Ibid.

11. Richard A. Linke and Paul S. Henry, "Coherent Optical Detection: A Thousand Calls on One Circuit," *IEEE Spectrum* (Institute of Electrical and Electronic Engineers, February 1987), p. 52.

12. Carter George, "Look to the Stars," *UNIX Review* (January 1986), pp. 55-62.

13. P. Bruce Berra and Nikos B. Troullinos, "Optical Techniques and Data/ Knowledge Base Machines," *Computer* (Institute of Electrical and Electronic Engineers, October 1987), p. 59.

14. Ibid., p. 61.

15. Ibid., p. 67.

16. Emily T. Smith, "An Optical Memory That Can Be Wiped Clean," *Business Week* (June 15, 1987), pp. 56-58.

17. Richard Snodgrass and Iisoo Ahn, "Temporal Databases," *Computer* (Institute of Electrical and Electronic Engineers, September1986), pp. 35-42.

18. Craig Stanfill and Brewster Kahle, "Parallel Free-Text Search on the Connection Machine System," *Communications of the ACM* (The Association for Computing Machinery, Vol. 29, No. 12, December 1986), p. 1230.

19. S.K.M. Wong and Wojciech Ziarko, "A Concept-Learning Information Retrieval System—Basic Ideas," *SIGIR Forum* (Special Interest Group on Information Retrieval of the Association for Computing Machinery, Spring-Summer 1986), pp. 16-17.

20. Lee Mantelman, "AI Carves Inroads: Network Design, Testing, and Management," *Data Communications* (July 1986), p. 109.

21. Ibid., p. 115.

22. Ibid., p. 116.

23. Ibid., p. 120.

24. Ibid., p. 109.

25. Wendy Goldman Rohm, "A Remote Promise," *Infosystems* (September 1986), pp. 54-56.

26. Bir Bhanu, "CAD-Based Robot Vision," *Computer* (Institute of Electrical and Electronic Engineers, August 1987), p. 13.

27. Ibid., p. 15.

7

Appendix: A Review of the Fundamentals

The following introduction to computers was written by Blake White in 1983 for technical literacy seminars held by the National Technical Association. It appeared in the January 1985 edition of *The Journal of the National Technical Association* and is reprinted here with permission. This provides a basic overview to the technology and terminology for readers not acquainted with the fundamentals of computer hardware, software, their history, and applications.

The cliché *computer revolution* has become an all-too-common and overused term. Trite or not, it indeed portrays the rapid, widespread, and overwhelming impact that the computer has had upon modern society. No technology has had such a broad range of potential applications in the home and workplace, nor such an impact on the way we interact and think.

The computer and its associated microelectronics industries have "ushered in the second industrial revolution," according to the National Academy of Sciences[1] and initiated the "Third Wave," as coined by futurist Alvin Toffler.[2] The emphasis of both statements is the totality of the impact of this new technology. The computer has become such an integral part of our lives that we now face the reality of this tool's capability to allow us not only to use it to simplify and speed up tasks, but to reorganize our view of the world. In fact, we are actually in the process of organizing our lives around the computer.

The pervasive computer finds itself in the workplace and the home and in the entertainment, transportation, communication, and medical arenas. At work, the computer produces jobless growth. Specifically, its employment implications extend well beyond the direct impact of automation of traditional blue-collar jobs by robots to the labor-saving, high-productivity improvements that computers provide for white-collar service and retail positions. The computer's ability to create economic growth without creating jobs is the key to its productivity. By doing a task faster, serving more customers with fewer people, the computer structurally changes the available jobs.

Department stores use electronic cash registers tied into their central computers to automatically check credit, process sales, record transactions, and manage inventory. Such tasks as stock recording and bookkeeping are greatly simplified. Electronic scanners instantly read universal product codes (UPC) on goods, thereby speeding up check-out lines at grocery stores. Optical scanners are connected to a central computer that measures stock levels and changes prices without needing clerks to mark every item. In the office, word processors (display typewriters with computer memories) speed up many facets of office work from typing reports to answering letters.

Word processors allow the typist to look at a document on a screen before it is printed and make any needed corrections. When corrections are required, only the incorrect words are changed, rather than the entire document. Such new office machines allow fewer workers to produce more documents, thus improving productivity and changing the nature of work.

At home, computers are bringing newspapers from all over the world within a keystroke of the personal computer owner. No longer need we worry about a rain-soaked or dog-chewed newspaper. Microcomputers display text on video screens similar to televisions. They also transmit and receive electronic mail, keep telephone listings, dial phone numbers until the party answers, monitor home security systems, such as burglar and fire alarms, automatically call authorities, and control heating and air conditioning systems in the most cost-effective and comfortable manner. Besides the familiar video games, computers are bringing self-paced, self-taught instruction into the home. From children's ABCs and sentence formation to learning Spanish, from basic counting to calculus, home computers are demonstrating the ability to do quite a bit more than shoot down cartoon aliens.

Computers are influencing our lives from the way we bank and shop at home to the way we store recipes and remember birthdays. They monitor the fuel mix in cars, monitor bodily functions in hospitals, simulate the yields from test plots for farmers, and reserve theater seats. The computer's ability to automate routine tasks gives us more time to think, create, and enjoy life. Its acceptance of our delegation of control of fire protection lets us rest easier. Its ability to correlate huge masses of data could, if used correctly, allow us to make better decisions. Its cost-effectiveness could also make current jobs obsolete. In either case, computers are tools! No more, no less. As such, they can be used for positive or negative aims. Their inherent capability for enrichment is also their capability for abuse. Positively or negatively, computers are here to stay.

The pervasiveness of computers in our society is a recent phenomenon. The Space Race, with its drive toward miniaturization, spawned a spin-off microelectronics industry that, contrary to most industries, produced products that actually declined in price. As an example, consider the computer-automobile analogy: If the auto industry had developed like the computer business, a Rolls Royce would now cost $2.75 and run 3 million miles on a gallon of gas.[3] Or consider the airline analogy: If the aircraft industry had evolved as spectacularly as the computer industry over the past twenty-five years, a Boeing 767 would now cost $500, and it would circle the globe in twenty minutes on five gallons of fuel.[4] The cost of computers is falling at a rate of 25 percent per year, and the cost of data storage at a rate of 40 percent annually. Computational speed has increased by a factor of 200; and in the last quarter century, the cost, energy consumption, and size of computers of comparable power have decreased by a factor of 10,000.

The result is the personal computer (PC). From the $5 calculator, equivalent to a room-sized computer of the 1940s, to the $500 microcomputer—which gives the same basic computing power as did a mainframe computer in the early 1960s—our society is becoming bombarded with cheap but useful marvels of microelectronics.

Twenty years ago the cost of a computer could be justified only if the machine met the needs of a large organization. Colleges, the military, and large corporations were the sole owners of such expensive machines. Today's personal computer can serve as a workstation for the individual. Moreover, just as it has become financially attractive to provide individuals with computers, so technical developments have made the human interface increasingly friendly. As such, a wide array of functions are now accessible to people with no technical background.

Technical literacy (or computer literacy) has become the catchword of the eighties. At first, computers were for the priestly class that could read and write complicated computer programs. Today, we seem to be in a stage in which the computer is so simple and inexpensive that the masses can use it without having to understand how it works. They can thus participate in computer literacy without necessarily being part of the electronic elite themselves. It has become no more necessary for the mass of people to understand how a computer works than it is to understand the mechanics of the internal combustion engine in order to drive a car.

The two key factors—decreasing costs and ease of use—are the driving forces behind the computer revolution. This revolution requires a widespread reformulation of the meaning of literacy. We are on the verge of an era in which the ability to read and write may not be sufficient to define what it is to be literate. "Literacy may soon mean being able to access, manipulate and store information in a computer," according to Benjamin Compaine writing for *Science Digest*.[5]

Some of these changes are already showing up in the job market. A study shows that jobs in the help wanted ads in the *New York Times* that required some form of computer literacy doubled between 1977 and 1982. For example, none of the listings for travel agents in 1977 mentioned the need for any computer-related skills, but five years later, 71 percent required the ability to operate computer-based reservation systems.[6] With this in mind, America is scrambling to become computer literate.

The first personal computer was put on the market in 1975 (although electronic hobby kits existed well before then). By the end of 1982, more than 1 million PCs were in service in the United States alone. In 1981, total sales of PCs and their accessories in the United States amounted to $2.2 billion, and sales are expected to surpass $6 billion by 1985.[7] Parents are taking out large loans to ensure their children's futures by purchasing home systems, and college computer science classes have lengthy waiting lists.

With all the hype about computers and their revolutionary impact, let's examine this remarkable device and its evolution.

THE HISTORY SO FAR

The development of the computer, as we know it, has a brief history indeed; however, the computer in its broadest sense has evolved with mathematics since the earliest recorded ages of humanity. Because people needed to measure wealth by the size of their flocks of sheep or herds of cattle, counting developed. Counting is so fundamental that we take it for granted. Early civilizations needed to know that ten cows are more than eight and, more basic, that ten cows and ten sheep may not be exactly equal— qualitative differences must be taken into consideration.

So early cultures developed sophisticated mathematical systems. The African societies of Babylon, Sumeria, and Egypt, the American nations of the Mayans, and the brilliance of the Chinese all demonstrated advanced numerical systems. With a system of counting there evolved a unique means of recording and enhancing the process and results of such mathematical schemes. Pebbles, ropes with knots, sticks, and written systems developed to supplement the ten fingers and toes that were the computers of the day.

To the best of our knowledge, the first device that can legitimately be called a computer is the abacus. Developed by the Chinese at least 2,500 years ago, the abacus proved that numbers could be handled more easily by sliding little beads on strings.[8] The procedure was complex, in that it required several steps and physical manipulation of beads to do simple arithmetic, but the efficiency and accuracy of the abacus cannot be denied. Even today, clerks in banks in the Far East check the results given by calculators with an abacus. Studies show that an adept abacus operator can be as fast and as accurate with either electronic calculator or abacus.[9] It is far more than a childish toy.

The same programmable concept—that of a general-purpose machine that can be told to do an almost infinite variety of similar tasks—was later seen in the weaving machines of the Industrial Revolution. The famous Jacquard loom, invented in 1800, used cards with patterns of holes to program a loom to produce patterns in fabric.[10] The same principle was used in player pianos. The piano never changed, but the songs could be programmed on a revolving wheel or set of rubber belts with the positions of the holes determining the song to be played.

In the United States, a young engineer named Herman Hollerith persuaded the Census Bureau to try the punched-card (programmable) idea in the 1870 census. The same process as used by the Jacquard loom was used to automate and summarize such personal information as age, sex, marital status, and race. The data encoded on punched cards was read by electronic sensors and tabulated. Hollerith's equipment worked so well that the Census Bureau's clerks occasionally turned it off to protect their jobs. Soon punched data on cards were widely used in office machinery, including that made by a small firm that absorbed Hollerith's company and became the International Business Machines Corporation, better known as IBM.[11]

Computers continued to evolve as the pressures of war and the economics of business demanded. The wartime needs for calculation of trajectories of bombs and the enormous analytical requirements of code breakers led to the solution of the fundamental computer problem. The greatest stumbling block in refining the mechanical computer was the enormous number of moving parts it required. During World War II, technical breakthroughs allowed vacuum tubes to replace mechanical parts as switches and gates in modern computers, thus speed and accuracy were drastically increased.[12]

Among the new breed of computers were Colossus I, designed in England by Alan Turing to break enemy codes and ENIAC (Electronic Numerical Integrator and Calculator) developed at the University of Pennsylvania in 1945 to calculate bomb trajectories.[13]

ENIAC manipulated complex equations describing interactions among velocity, mass, air resistance, and gravity. After the war, it was adapted to perform other functions, thus becoming a general-purpose computer.

The advantage of these early electronic computers was that they could operate much more quickly than their electromagnetic or mechanical cousins but were bulky, power hungry, and unreliable. ENIAC, for example, covered 3,000 cubic feet, weighed 30 tons, contained 18,000 vacuum tubes, and was difficult to keep going more than a few minutes at a time.[14] It also required an air conditioner of roughly the same size to cool it.

In many ways, ENIAC and Colossus were the first machines to qualify as computers in the sense that we use the term today. The gulf that separates them from modern machines was widened in 1947 as a team of scientists at Bell Laboratories in New Jersey invented the first transistor.[15] A transistor contains materials that conduct electricity only at appropriate electronic signals, and, as such, the transistor does the same job as a vacuum tube. It can amplify signals, make them positive or negative, be used as relays with only the stable conditions of "on" or "off," and it can act as triggers, gates, or electronic latches. This combination of functions and their ability to operate in digital (on/off) mode made transistors the perfect replacement for tubes in computers.

The transistor has three great advantages over the tube. First, it is small— barely larger than a match head. Second, it is cheap to produce and uses less energy. Third, it is much more reliable. With these points in its favor, the transistor replaced the tube in 1956 as Bell built the first fully transistorized computer, the Leprechaun.

Since then, transistors have become even smaller and have been improved in their interactions. The small size enables many of them to be packed into a tiny space and also enhances the speed of their operation. Linking transistors allowed mass production of computer logic in circuit boards of transistors.

The fully integrated circuit is the descendant of the transistor. This device is manufactured in one operation and links as many as 250,000 transistors on a silicon chip of less than one-fourth inch square.

The cost of these chips has fallen dramatically. For a few cents, it is possible to buy a silicon chip containing all the power of ENIAC. The chip is not only more reliable but also much smaller and costs only a tiny fraction as much to run.[16]

The silicon chip is the secret behind today's microprocessors. The low cost of digital watches, stereo equipment, and personal computers is a direct result of the cheap microchip. Its high reliability and small size allow spacecraft to have multiple onboard computers. (Imagine trying to get ENIAC off the ground. There would have been no moon landing or even rockets and satellites with computers that size.) The microchip's vitality, flexibility, and energy efficiency is what makes the computer so revolutionary. For the first time, we have seized a technology that is relatively pollution free, miserly with energy, and seems to create more than it destroys.

ANATOMY OF A COMPUTER

A computer is essentially a machine that receives, stores, manipulates, and communicates data. It takes raw data, processes it, and generates information. The distinction being that *data* represent pure facts, and *information* is processed facts which give insight for some humanly useful purpose.

At the heart of the computer is the *central processing unit (CPU)*. This is the brain of the machine. It performs the basic arithmetic and logic functions and supervises the entire operation of the machine. Closely aligned to the CPU is the primary *memory* where both instructions and data can be stored, and other memory dedicated to controlling the *input* and *output* of the system. For example, a personal computer has a *read only memory (ROM)* which contains the computer's operating instructions (start up the computer, how to "read" in data, for example) and a *random access memory (RAM)* in which the instructions for the particular tasks the operator wants to be performed are stored. Memory is measured in *bytes* which are equivalent to one typed character. A byte is composed of *bits*, a series of electrical on/off codes that represent characters such as 1, A, B, d, ?, $, 8.

Most computers have a *keyboard*. This typewriterlike device is what is used to communicate with the CPU. Messages are sent to the computer via the keyboard. This input device is a cousin to *punched cards* and the modern electronic *scanners* at retail stores and grocery check-outs. Each input device communicates data and instructions to the CPU.

The CPU communicates to us via a *terminal*. Terminals can be paper printers or televisionlike screens called *monitors* or *CRTs (cathode ray tubes)*.

Large amounts of data are stored outside the computer on *magnetic disks or tapes*. Just as music is stored on albums or cassette tapes, data needed by the computer as *instructions (programs)* or as input data to be manipulated by the program can be stored on disks or magnetic tapes.

More sophisticated systems employ a *modem* and telephone lines to link a computer to other computers or disk drives with large amounts of data stored on disk drives (databases or data banks). Modems send and receive messages between computers and provide the novice and the professional access to the world of electronically stored information.

The CPU is physically composed of *silicon chips*. These chips and other electronic elements constitute the computer's *hardware*. The hardware can do nothing by itself. It requires an array of programs, collectively called *software*, to tell it exactly, step by step what to do. There are two kinds of software: the *operating system*, which controls the computer's operation and manages the flow of information, and the *application program*, which instructs the computer to perform specific tasks for the user like calculating a payroll, editing a letter, or solving an equation. The key point to remember is how absolutely stupid computers are. They are extremely fast, but this speed is applied to very simple tasks, over and over again. It is the program, written by a human, that instructs the computer. Without the program, all we have is a hunk of wires and a TV screen.

This is why we say a computer is merely a tool. It only does what it is told. Unfortunately, sometimes what it is told is wrong; it doesn't care. It will perform a wrong operation as quickly and as efficiently as a correct one. From this perspective, the program that we input to the computer is its weakest link. Programmers like to put it this way: "Garbage in equals garbage out." A computer cannot "think" per se. Whatever we tell it to do, it will do (if it is within its capabilities), no matter how incorrect our instructions.

So how does it work? What makes it tick? Mentioned earlier was the chip's ability to be seen as either on or off. Electricity is either flowing through it or not flowing at all. This *binary* state is the simplicity underlying computers. Remember the Jacquard loom's holes which represented the fabric pattern? This too was binary. It had either a hole or a solid piece of card for each section. The presence of a hole signified something to the machine. Well, the presence or absence of electric current can be arrayed in such a way that a sequence of on/off *semiconductors* can be coded to mean a particular number or letter of the alphabet—a byte. This is the first principle of computing. Letters, numbers, and symbols can be coded to be a series of on/off electrical switches recognizable by the computer. It performs its calculations and retranslates from its *machine language* back into letters and numbers for our use. The program acts as an interpreter between us and the computer. It translates human words into machine codes in a sequence used by the computer as instructions.

These instructions can be further simplified into four basic operations. All logic can be interpreted into a series of computer-recognizable instructions using the concepts of AND, OR, NOR, and NAND. AND tells the machine to do a series of things: do A, and do B, and do C. OR tells the system to do A or B, but not both. NOR instructs it not to do A or B. NAND tells the system not to do A and not to do B.[17] Computers are well versed in this kind of logic and can use it to perform a series of instructions.

The instructions themselves have three basic tasks that can be programmed: series, branch, and loop. A series procedure tells the computer to do A, then do B, then C, and so forth. The branch, however, tells the system to do A, then B, then skip C and go off and do procedures D, E, and F before going ahead and completing C. The loop instructs the computer to do process A, then B, then D until a condition specified by the programmer occurs (such as finding the right account number in a credit file). After meeting this condition, it can then proceed with step C. Graphically represented in Figure 7-1 are these three programming functions. By using combinations of these basic functions, the application program can instruct the computer to process data to search for a personnel record, update a charge account by adding a recent payment, sort a mailing list by alphabetical order or zip code, and monitor a chemical plant process until substance flows exceed a predefined limit, then signal the operator or automatically shut down the process.

Computers keep track of things. They sort things, add, subtract, and compare. That's all. The ability of computers to do these simple tasks extremely fast, usually in thousandths or millionths of a second, and do them for lengthy time periods that would bore any human is the beauty and the usefulness of them. The program is the language used to instruct the computer, in a step-by-step fashion, how a problem is to be solved or how data are retrieved.

Application programs can be written or purchased. With the software market exploding, good programs may be bought to satisfy almost any need. If not, programming a set of instructions is always an alternative. By breaking down complicated procedures into their simplest component parts and applying logic and the basic functions to it, writing a program can be as simple as translating a foreign language.

Some of the better-known and popular languages include *BASIC* for beginners and personal computer users and *FORTRAN* for scientific and engineering applications. FORTRAN usually runs on larger machines (although PCs are becoming powerful enough to process FORTRAN programs). *PASCAL* is popular for intermediate users because it gives the power of FORTRAN with the simplicity of BASIC. The business community typically uses older mainframe languages such as *COBOL* or a mature, yet viable, language such as *PL/1* for automating accounting procedures. Each of these languages is procedural in nature—in other words, the programmer must outline all of the steps needed to solve the problem.

Figure 7-1
Basic Logical Functions

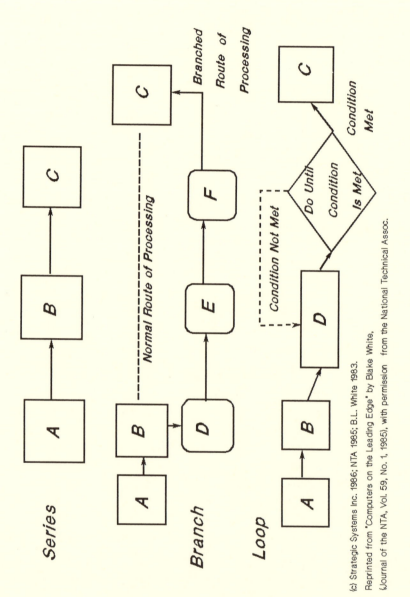

Other higher level, so-called *Fourth and Fifth Generation languages* are available. They are driven not by step-by-step instructions from the user, but by the user stating the output that is desired and the format of its presentation. The machine does the rest. These user-friendly languages are what is really driving widespread computer utilization. Their ease of use and short learning curves make them quite attractive for people who want to use a computer, but don't want to program one.

Bookstores and libraries provide hundreds of references on programming languages, and the reader is encouraged to seek them out. But the important point worth remembering is that a program is the instruction set that tells the computer what to do and how to do it. Without a program, the computer is a dead piece of machinery. The key component is the human who specifies the programming steps and brings the computer to the machine equivalent of life.

THE FUTURE

The computer is bound to revolutionize our society. As we become more dependent on its capabilities, we must constantly monitor against potential abuses. It would be an obscenity to let the tool that is the cutting edge of a high-tech future go the way of other less successful technologies—becoming more a nightmare than a dream. Only technically literate, involved, concerned people can bring forth the following potentials:

- *Supercomputers*, currently under development in Japan, could bring the accumulated knowledge of humanity together to solve problems. Their capabilities would be at everyone's fingertips, and they would be faster and represent a thousandfold improvement over current machines.[18]
- Computers are evolving that see, comprehend, and then respond to complex visual environments.[19]
- A *memory processor* in automobiles will tell the garage mechanic's computer the exact history of the events leading up to a malfunction. Presumably, it could also forewarn of problems.[20]
- The Drexel-Moss computer knee exploits the computer's capacity for unraveling the electrical impulse from the brain to help handicapped people walk.[21]
- Future Japanese cars will sound a sonar-initiated alarm as you back out of your driveway if the car comes within two yards of an object. Windshield wipers and headlights turn on automatically as it rains

or turns dark, respectively. Computer-controlled suspension will take account of and compensate for the distribution of passengers, and the *Navicom* program will outline a map of the city, directing you to your destination.[22]

- Satellite-based computers will manage worldwide air travel more effectively than humans can. By keeping track of every aircraft's longitude and latitude several times per second, computers could keep the skies safer for air travel.[23]

- Instantaneous language translators could break down our local prejudices and misunderstanding by allowing a person to communicate verbally in Swahili and be understood halfway around the world in English.

These are but a few of the computer's benefits. To say it is revolutionary is to understate its potential. Not only will it be part of a revolution, but it will be the leading edge of a revolution at work, at home, and at play.

NOTES

1. Colin Norman, "The New Industrial Revolution: How Microelectronics May Change the Workplace," *The Futurist* (The World Future Society, February 1981), pp. 30-40.

2. Alvin Toffler, *The Third Wave* (New York: William Morrow, 1980).

3. Otto Friedrich, "The Computer Moves In," *Time* (January 3, 1983), pp. 14-24.

4. H.D. Toong and Amar Gupta, "Personal Computers," *Scientific American* (December 1982), pp. 87-107.

5. Benjamin Compaine, "The New Literacy," *Science Digest* (March 1983), pp. 16-112.

6. Ibid.

7. Toong and Gupta, "Personal Computers," pp. 87-107.

8. Frederic Golden, "Big Dimwits and Little Geniuses," *Time* (January 3, 1983), pp. 30-32.

9. Gordon Pask and Susan Curran, *Micro Man* (London: Century, 1982), pp. 6-7.

10. James Burke, *Connections* (Boston: Little, Brown, 1978), pp. 111-17.

11. Golden, "Big Dimwits and Little Geniuses," pp. 30-32.

12. Pask and Curran, *Micro Man*, p. 18.

13. Ibid., pp. 18-19.

14. Ibid., pp. 18-22.

15. Ibid., p. 21.

16. Ibid., pp. 21-25.

17. Ralph J. Smith, *Circuits, Devices, and Systems*, 3rd ed. (New York: John Wiley and Sons, 1976), pp. 365-69.

18. Edward A. Feigenbaum and Pamela McCorduck, *The Fifth Generation* (Reading, Mass.: Addison Wesley, 1983).

19. "The Coming Generation of Supercomputers," *Science Digest* (March 1983), pp. 73-81.

20. Ibid.

21. Ibid.

22. Ibid.

23. Ibid.

Index

About the Author

BLAKE L. WHITE is President and Principal Consultant of Strategic Systems, Inc., a San Francisco-based technology assessment consulting firm. His experience in the computer industry includes positions with Procter & Gamble and Hewlett-Packard as a systems analyst, designer, database administrator, support manager, operations manager, systems integrator, industry analyst, data communications product manager, researcher, and senior consultant. He has contributed journal articles on computers, space industrialization, energy alternatives, and technical literacy.